PRAIS

MW01244404

"In *Changed Eyes,* Fr. Joel Huffstetler, an artist of both the spoken and written word, shares his deep personal and pastoral reflections on the challenges facing us during these difficult times. His writing style in this engaging set of biblical meditations is personal as he speaks of his experiences, and scholarly in his contemplation and application of ancient biblical stories. In the book, he reflects on how we can move toward physical, spiritual and cultural healing. *Changed Eyes* is an immersive, relevant, and comforting reading experience, just what we all need in this day and age."

—*Brenda Orcutt, member, Oil Painters of America, American Impressionist Society, and American Women Artists*

"It is never enough for preachers just to preach the gospel. They must make it heard. This requires imagination, sensitivity, and the determination never to make the complex into something dishonestly simple. In this book, Joel Huffstetler shows he has these necessary qualities in abundance. Reminding us of the importance of difficulty in life, as a place where walls break down and distilled freshness can break through, he takes us into the heart and the hope of Christian faith."

—*Mark Oakley, Dean of St John's College, University of Cambridge*

"In these sermons which are at once challenging and comforting, Joel Huffstetler brings the Bible to bear on the complex circumstances of global pandemic and racial conflict. He shows that by wrestling with Scripture our perspectives can change and we can find resources for hopefulness and lessons for loving one another in our troubled world. This is preaching at its best: thoughtful, clear, and concise."

—*Mark D. Chapman, Professor of the History of Modern Theology, University of Oxford*

"Throughout *Changed Eyes*, Joel Huffstetler lovingly and eloquently reminds us that moments of crisis—global pandemics, racial reckonings, political discord—also present moments of opportunity, in this case, the opportunity to realize anew the grace and love that Jesus Christ offers a broken world."

—*Jeffrey M. Ringer, Associate Professor of English, University of Tennessee*

"Would that all churches were fortunate enough to have a truth-teller of this caliber, someone who can see the truth in a text and present it in such a memorable way."

—*Carl R. Holladay, Charles Howard Candler Professor Emeritus of New Testament, Candler School of Theology, Emory University*

CHANGED EYES

PANDEMIC, PROTESTS, PROCLAMATION

JOEL W. HUFFSTETLER

APOCRYPHILE
PRESS

THE APOCRYPHILE PRESS
PO Box 255, Hannacroix, NY 12087

Copyright © 2023 by Joel Huffstetler
ISBN 978-1-958061-24-4 / paperback
ISBN 978-1-958061-25-1 / ebook

Cover image, *Transitions in Life,* Oil on Canvas, by Brenda Orcutt
www.orcuttfineart.com

Please join our mailing list at
www.apocryphilepress.com/free
We'll keep you up to date on all our new releases,
and we'll also invite you to download a FREE BOOK.
Visit us today!

For Debbie

CONTENTS

Foreword   ix
Carl R. Holladay

Preface   xi

Introduction   xiii
The Right Rev. Brian L. Cole

1. Her Achievement Is Remarkable   1
2. Out of the Dark, and Into the Light   8
3. Changed Eyes   12
4. A Servant's Heart   20
5. The Bonds of Christian Community   25
6. The Vital Importance of Christian Community   29
7. Having New Eyes   34
8. Once You Label Me, You Negate Me   39
9. What Matters Most   44
10. The Prison of My Own Creation   50
11. The Single Garment of Destiny   56
12. The Portrait of God We Call the Trinity   62
13. Gut-level Compassion   68
14. Our Remedy Is the Grace of Christ   73
15. Different Facets of God's Glory   78
16. The Living Tablets of Our Hearts   83
17. For There Is No Distinction   88
18. Holding Her Ground   93
19. The World of Grace   99
20. A Love That Is Not Easy   105
21. An Extraordinary Portrait of Grace   109
22. The Wideness of God's Mercy   114
23. Gotta Serve Somebody   119
24. A Living Text   124
25. The Joyful Service of Those In Need   130
26. Systemic Injustices All Around   137
27. A Mix of Pain and Hope   142
28. Truly I Tell You   147

29. Attention   153
30. In Memory of Tyler Herndon   159
31. It Makes A Difference What You Believe   164

   Acknowledgments   171
   Notes   173
   Bibliography   183
   About the Author   193

FOREWORD
CARL R. HOLLADAY

Biblical preaching is a two-way street. It relates the Bible to people but also relates people to the Bible. In times of crisis the preacher's task is to find biblical texts that can speak to the uneasiness and fears created by social and political turmoil, or by a global pandemic of unprecedented magnitude. But the preacher must also point people to the Bible, showing how it can sustain them in times of trouble.

The Bible has been a source of strength and consolation for centuries. Somehow, people of faith have always found themselves turning to the Bible for guidance and encouragement. But it is not always easy to find the right passage or to discern God's Word within a passage. This is where ministers of the Word have a special responsibility. They are called to use their training, along with their ministerial experience and their spiritual resources that have been cultivated over many years, to assist members of their congregations in not only listening *to* the Word, but also listening *for* the Word that is mediated through the biblical text.

These sermons were delivered in an Episcopal Church in East Tennessee during 2020, a year of multiple crises both national and international. Preaching to his congregation during this turbulent year, Joel Huffstetler displays a rare ability to connect text and people. He is able to see how a specific text spoke to its ancient readers but also how it can speak to modern readers. He presents his listeners with a biblical text, first by reading it aloud, then exploring and probing it, wrestling with it, and moving through it in a way that is genuinely illuminating.

What commends these sermons is their directness. Huffstetler's clear, simple, yet well-crafted, powerful prose reflects a commendable honesty and transparency. Carefully selected quotes from a range of commentators and other writers reflect extensive research and reading, but these are interwoven with Joel's own exegetical insights. His own interpretation comes through clearly, as does the way in which his pastoral experience informs his preaching.

Coping with multiple crises in 2020, parishioners were eager to hear a message of hope and encouragement. They wanted to hear the truth about the pandemic and the ways it challenged their congregational solidarity. They also wanted to hear about the social and political stresses on display during every news cycle. But they also wanted to be reassured that the seams binding them together were strong enough to endure, that the church's faith—and faithfulness—could be an anchor in a time of storm.

Would that all churches were fortunate enough to have a truth-teller of this caliber, someone who can see the truth in a text and present it in such a memorable way.

Carl R. Holladay, PhD
Charles Howard Candler Professor Emeritus of New Testament
Candler School of Theology, Emory University

PREFACE

The biblical meditations contained within this book were first offered from mid-March 2020 through to the end of that year—in the thick of the global pandemic. Most were offered as Sunday sermons, though some were brief homilies for mid-week services of worship, and others were podcast talks. All have been revised for publication. The addresses dating from mid-March through to mid-September were offered online, as in-person worship was suspended due to the pandemic. From mid-September on, limited in-person worship was allowed with carefully formulated safety protocols in place, though the majority of worshippers remained online.

One of the great biblical theologians of the twentieth century, Karl Barth, memorably observed that, in preparing a sermon, a preacher should have the Bible in one hand and a newspaper in the other. The addresses in this book were crafted to speak *from* the Bible *to* the moment at hand, the first global pandemic in one hundred years, and, as of the late spring and summer of 2020, the tsunami of social protests following the deaths of Ahmaud Arbery and George Floyd. At the same time, they were crafted to be forward looking, urging both preacher and listener to search out the enduring lessons embedded within the events of 2020.

No sane person would have chosen to experience the pain, the suffering, the dislocations, the uncertainties—the myriad losses—of 2020. That said, those of us who survived have before us now, and for the remainder of our lives, the question: In the aftermath of 2020, do we see the world, and each other, with changed eyes?

Joel W. Huffstetler
Rector, St. Luke's Episcopal Church
Cleveland, Tennessee
November 22, 2022

INTRODUCTION
THE RIGHT REV. BRIAN L. COLE

"Preacher, give us a word!"

You, good reader, have before you the words of a preacher who was preparing and preaching these sermons in what was repeatedly said to be unprecedented times.

While they were offered in a time of global upset on numerous fronts, as these are sermons deeply rooted in the biblical story, we come to understand that, in reality, no time is unprecedented. We have been here before. And, as long as our Lord tarries, we will be here again. So, what can the Word, which heals and confronts and judges and saves, say to God's people in troubled times?

I am grateful that Fr. Joel Huffstetler continues to practice his vocation as preacher, teacher, priest, and pastor. These sermons proclaim the Good News in a time when there were daily updates of bad and troubling news. They teach us how to live faithfully in the times in which we are situated. These sermons possess a sacramental quality to them, with grace abounding and made known to those who can hear what is said and see what is shown.

Finally, Fr. Joel is a pastor to all, not simply the members of

xiv THE RIGHT REV. BRIAN L. COLE

St. Luke's Episcopal Church, Cleveland, Tennessee, on Broad Street, but to the wider community of Cleveland and beyond. Fr. Joel, on more than one occasion, has shown me the city of Cleveland, not only the Chamber of Commerce-quality streets near St Luke's, but also the often forgotten and ignored parts of his city, which he has neither forgotten nor ignored.

Reading these sermons which were preached during the time of pandemic emergency in our country and world, I was reminded of Henry Stout's book, *Upon the Altar of the Nation: A Moral History of the Civil War*. Stout's book examines closely the sermons delivered from Northern and Southern pulpits during the U. S. Civil War of 1861 to 1865. In the actual days of the hot fighting, how were preachers either addressing or ignoring the events of their day? Considering those days, what theological reflections were being offered or ideas defended?

Years from now, when historians of Covid times will look back to see how the Church, through the faithful work of this one preacher and pastor, addressed both his people and the times in which they lived, they will find a document worth commending. These sermons speak to the moment and to the people living in those moments. In a time when many were at a loss for how to address what was before us, Fr. Joel continued to embrace a belief that the biblical story had a word for us, and that the pulpit remained a primary place for standing.

I recently attended a public lecture which referenced a book on preaching from the early twentieth century. The book being referenced was *Positive Preaching and Modern Mind*, by the Scottish theologian P. T. Forsyth. The book was compiled from Forsyth's Lyman Beecher Lectures on Preaching, given at Yale University in 1907. The lecture I heard in 2022 quoted the following from Forsyth's 1907 lecture: "We must all preach *to* our age, but woe to us if it is our age we preach."

Fr. Joel's sermons heed the words of Forsyth. They spoke *to* the moment. They avoided, however, speaking *from* the moment in such a way that did not transcend the moment. In a time where vision was lacking, Fr. Joel's sermons helped his people see that the Suffering Servant is still the one we are to follow.

The Right Rev. Brian L. Cole
Fifth Bishop of the Episcopal Diocese of East Tennessee

CHAPTER ONE
HER ACHIEVEMENT IS REMARKABLE

Thursday in the Third Week of Lent
19 March 2020 • John 4:5-42

⁵ So [Jesus] came to a Samaritan city called Sychar, near the plot of ground that Jacob had given to his son Joseph. ⁶ Jacob's well was there, and Jesus, tired out by his journey, was sitting by the well. It was about noon. ⁷ A Samaritan woman came to draw water, and Jesus said to her, "Give me a drink." ⁸ (His disciples had gone to the city to buy food.) ⁹ The Samaritan woman said to him, "How is it that you, a Jew, ask a drink of me, a woman of Samaria?" (Jews do not share things in common with Samaritans.) ¹⁰ Jesus answered her, "If you knew the gift of God, and who it is that is saying to you, 'Give me a drink,' you would have asked him, and he would have given you living water." ¹¹ The woman said to him, "Sir, you have no bucket, and the well is deep. Where do you get that living water? ¹² Are you greater than our ancestor Jacob, who gave us the well, and with his sons and his flocks drank from it?" ¹³ Jesus said to her, "Everyone who drinks of this water will be thirsty again, ¹⁴ but those who drink of the water that I will give them will never be

2 JOEL W. HUFFSTETLER

thirsty. The water that I will give will become in them a spring of water gushing up to eternal life." [15] The woman said to him, "Sir, give me this water, so that I may never be thirsty or have to keep coming here to draw water." [16] Jesus said to her, "Go, call your husband, and come back." [17] The woman answered him, "I have no husband." Jesus said to her, "You are right in saying, 'I have no husband'; [18] for you have had five husbands, and the one you have now is not your husband. What you have said is true!" [19] The woman said to him, "Sir, I see that you are a prophet. [20] Our ancestors worshiped on this mountain, but you say that the place where people must worship is in Jerusalem." [21] Jesus said to her, "Woman, believe me, the hour is coming when you will worship the Father neither on this mountain nor in Jerusalem. [22] You worship what you do not know; we worship what we know, for salvation is from the Jews.

[23] But the hour is coming, and is now here, when the true worshipers will worship the Father in spirit and truth, for the Father seeks such as these to worship him. [24] God is spirit, and those who worship him must worship in spirit and truth." [25] The woman said to him, "I know that Messiah is coming" (who is called Christ). "When he comes, he will proclaim all things to us." [26] Jesus said to her, "I am he, the one who is speaking to you." [27] Just then his disciples came. They were astonished that he was speaking with a woman, but no one said, "What do you want?" or, "Why are you speaking with her?" [28] Then the woman left her water jar and went back to the city. She said to the people, [29] "Come and see a man who told me everything I have ever done! He cannot be the Messiah, can he?" [30] They left the city and were on their way to him. [31] Meanwhile the disciples were urging him, "Rabbi, eat something." [32] But he said to them, "I have food to eat that you do not know about." [33] So the disciples said to one another, "Surely no one has brought him something to eat?" [34] Jesus said to them, "My food is to do the will of him who sent me and to complete his work. [35] Do you

not say, 'Four months more, then comes the harvest'? But I tell you, look around you, and see how the fields are ripe for harvesting. [36] The reaper is already receiving wages and is gathering fruit for eternal life, so that sower and reaper may rejoice together. [37] For here the saying holds true, 'One sows and another reaps.' [38] I sent you to reap that for which you did not labor. Others have labored, and you have entered into their labor." [39] Many Samaritans from that city believed in him because of the woman's testimony, "He told me everything I have ever done." [40] So when the Samaritans came to him, they asked him to stay with them; and he stayed there two days. [41] And many more believed because of his word. [42] They said to the woman, "It is no longer because of what you said that we believe, for we have heard for ourselves, and we know that this is truly the Savior of the world."

It is often said these days that we are losing the art of conversation. I happen to be one of the people saying it. We *are* losing the art of conversation.

Technology has many good uses. I do embrace good, constructive uses of technology. Oftentimes we think in terms of technology making things easier and faster, but when we put so much emphasis on making communication easier, faster and more 'efficient,' we risk losing opportunities to have relaxed, leisurely, free-flowing conversations with each other. In recent years, I have noticed how often people will say after ten or fifteen minutes: "I don't want to take up too much of your time." My typical response is: "I am in no hurry."

The art of conversation is crucially important to us. We must retain and cultivate the ability to talk to one another. Jesus and the Samaritan woman offer a model conversation for us in John 4.

Unfortunately, technology that is supposed to make communication easier is often weaponized. We lob 'Twitter bombs' at each other. The ready access to technology, and its relative anonymity, leads to many coarse and unproductive uses. Veteran legislators in both Parliament (United Kingdom) and our Congress have recently stated that dialogue among our elected leaders is "coarser" now. This is a reality with which we have to come to grips. We must relearn how to communicate constructively and have conversation that is mutually respectful. We have a new phrase in our lexicon as of the last few years: "He (or she) has taken down the Tweet." And so often we hear the term: "He (or she) has had to walk that back." We have to 'walk back' careless, imprecise use of language, which oftentimes contains untruths. Conversely, Jesus and the Samaritan woman model for us the *art* of conversation. We have much to learn from John 4:5-42.

When I was in graduate school at Candler School of Theology, Emory University, Fred Craddock (1928-2015) was in his prime as one of our great American preachers. My attendance in chapel at Candler was not exemplary, with one notable exception—when Dr. Craddock was preaching! To this day I can remember many of Dr. Craddock's punchlines. All these years later, I can still hear the tone of his voice.

In a sermon on John 4:5-42, Fred Craddock states that there are three essential elements to a conversation. The *first* element is that we must recognize the differences between us as individuals.[1] We all come from a different 'place,' we have different backgrounds, different life experiences. However similar we may seem on the surface, we all have been shaped by our unique mixture of life experiences. Craddock makes the point that for conversation to be meaningful we have to recognize and respect our different points of view.

The Danish philosopher and theologian Søren Kierkegaard (1813-55) said: "Once you label me, you negate me." The insight here is that when we attach a label to someone we stop dealing with them in their individuality. It is a brilliant insight.

Once you *label* me, you *negate* me. Craddock urges us to recognize the differences that exist between us, and the individuality in play in a conversation.

The *second* essential element in conversation is that amidst our differences we must yet recognize what we have in common.² We must recognize our *common humanity*. Even though it is essential that we recognize differences, in order to have a meaningful conversation we must look for common ground—for what binds us together despite our differences. A part of our losing the art of conversation is losing our sense of commonality, our sense of a shared common destiny. In some extreme instances, even our common humanity seems in question these days! We must recognize and remember what we share in common to be able to communicate meaningfully with each other.

The *third* essential element of a conversation for Craddock is that we must be open to change.³ If we are not just going to talk *at* each other, or *past* each other, we must be open to change. In a conversation, we may be 99.9% convinced of our position, but at least 0.1% of us has to be open to change for a conversation to be all that it can be.

The English priest and spiritual writer Michael Mayne (1929-2006) once observed about people who talk *at* each other or *past* each other—people who speak without listening—that such interaction is simply "a disturbance of the air." It is merely a disturbance of the air when we are talking past each other rather than engaging one another in meaningful, interactive conversation that has at least the potential to change us, to change how we see things.

John 4 contains the longest recorded conversation of Jesus in the Gospels. In 4:5-42 we have on offer the most sustained dialogue between Jesus and one other person in the Gospels, and thus the conversation is crucially important for this reason alone, but for many other reasons as well. And the conversation was unlikely. A Samaritan woman interacting with a Galilean Jewish male would have been deemed socially improper. John 4:9 reads: "The Samaritan woman said to him, 'How is it that you, a Jew, ask a drink of me, a woman of Samaria?'" The mere possibility of this conversation was unlikely, indeed, forbidden, and yet it serves as a great example of how an unlikely pairing of conversation partners can yield fruit. Jesus' disciples appear in the narrative in verse 27, and John says of them: "They were astonished that he was speaking with a woman..." A Samaritan woman speaking to a Jewish male was not a politically correct conversation in their first-century world; nevertheless, Jesus and the woman enter into a meaningful dialogue.

In commenting on this interaction, Gail O'Day notes that Jesus and the woman cross "...the boundary between male and female, the boundary between 'chosen people' and 'rejected people.'"[4] And, "Jesus' journey to Samaria and his conversation with the woman demonstrate that the grace of God that he offers is available to all."[5] Jesus frequently crosses boundaries. Again and again in the Gospels we see Jesus breaking down barriers that humans have erected. What a marvelous example we have here in John 4 of what can happen when an unlikely conversation is entered into in good faith, and with openness of mind.

Verses 17-18 deal with the woman's marital history. She has had five husbands, and her current partner is not her husband. This woman has been stereotyped over the years and judged harshly, and yet, refreshingly, one searches in vain for any words of judgment about the woman's character coming from Jesus. Jesus does not *judge* this woman; he enters into a conversation with her. Commentators over the years have speculated, wildly in some cases, and often times unkindly, about this woman's marital history, to which Gail O'Day responds: "...the reasons for the woman's marital history intrigue commentators, but do not seem to concern Jesus."[6] Jesus meets this woman where she is, without judgment, and simply engages her in conversation. What a lastingly important example we have here regarding meeting people where they are, with the hope that we are extended the same courtesy.

What we have here in John 4:5-42 is a marvelous reminder of what can happen when human beings talk *with* one another and *to* one another with openness of mind—when we actually listen to another person's point of view and are open to it influencing our own stance going forward.

Our passage offers such a useful picture of a fruitful conversation. John writes in verse 39: "Many Samaritans from that city believed in him because of the woman's testimony, 'He told me everything I have ever done.'" What happens subsequently in the passage is that the villagers themselves go out to Jesus and respond to him for themselves. So not only does the woman's testimony bring others into an *awareness* of Jesus—it also opens the door for them to develop their own relationship with him.

Susan E. Hylen has written about the Samaritan woman: "Her achievement is remarkable."[7] And Robert Kysar observes: "Because of her the reader of the Gospel knows that no matter who you are—no matter what your stature in society may be—the revelation of God in Christ is for you!"[8] Amen.

CHAPTER TWO

OUT OF THE DARK, AND INTO THE LIGHT

Fourth Sunday in Lent
22 March 2020 • John 9:1-5

[1] As he walked along, he saw a man blind from birth. [2] His disciples asked him, "Rabbi, who sinned, this man or his parents, that he was born blind?" [3] Jesus answered, "Neither this man nor his parents sinned; he was born blind so that God's works might be revealed in him. [4] We must work the works of him who sent me while it is day; night is coming when no one can work. [5] As long as I am in the world, I am the light of the world."

In John 9:2 we read: "Rabbi, who sinned, this man or his parents, that he was born blind?" *Why* was this man born blind? There are examples in Hebrew Scriptures of a theology which holds that the sins of one generation are visited upon another. We see examples of this theology in Exodus, in the Psalter, and in Isaiah. But in Ezekiel 18 the prophet explicitly rejects this idea, making the point that the sins of previous generations are *not* visited upon their descendants. Theology is always evolving.

John 9:1 reads: "As he [Jesus] walked along, he saw a man blind from birth." And so the disciples ask: "Rabbi, who sinned, this man or his parents, that he was born blind?" Simply put: *Why?* In addition to *Why?* we oftentimes ask: *What?* What should our response be to a given situation? What does *this* moment, *this* situation, require? The disciples ask a question and invite discussion: Tell us, Teacher, why does this have to be? Jesus responds not with a talking point, but with action.

In this moment in our culture, amidst an emerging global pandemic, it is perfectly natural and normal—and, ultimately, productive—to ask: Why? Why this outbreak? How has this happened? Why (or how) are we not better prepared? These are legitimate questions. Ultimately, it is incumbent upon us to understand how this did happen. Also, we must learn from this outbreak of COVID-19 how to be better prepared in the future. So Why? is a valid question. But Why? has to be balanced by What? What does this moment require of us? What can we *do* to flatten the curve?

There are two basic things we all can do. You have heard it in the press, you have heard it from our national, state, and local leaders, and now you are hearing it in church. First, wash your hands, frequently and thoroughly, for at least twenty seconds. The second thing we can do is social distancing. The nature of this worship service reflects our new reality. A handful of us are here in the church building offering 'public' worship. We know that we are being joined by many others online. As we worship today, we are *practicing* social distancing. In the end, our faith always is meant to lead us to action. We may ask: Why? But we balance Why? with What? What is our response to this emerging pandemic? What are best practices in this new season?

In John 9:5 we read: "As long as I am in the world, I am the light of the world." Here we encounter an important piece of Johannine theology in this image of Jesus as the light of the world. We are right to ask: What? What is our response? What can *we* do? What can *I* do as an individual? As people of faith, our response is to be grounded in and guided by the teachings and the Spirit of Christ—the light of the world.

While listening to the radio this past week I heard an elected official here in the state of Tennessee say: "Right now, we need the public to be calm." He then went on to say: "We need churches, houses of worship, to show leadership in helping people to be calm." Churches, houses of worship, are asked to respond to this new season of social distancing calmly and compassionately, understanding that in this evolving and uncertain situation fear is real and is an understandable response to so much that is unknown. And yet this fear is best met with calmness and steadiness.

The clergy of the diocese had a Zoom call on Friday with our bishop, and he made the wise and helpful comment that this new season is more a marathon than a sprint. We do not know how long this need for social distancing will last. But we do know that it will pass.

We find ourselves in the early stages of a marathon, not a sprint. But a marathon does have an end point. As challenging as the length of a marathon is, it does, ultimately, come to an end. Our response to this unwanted marathon has to be undertaken step by step, 'mile by mile,' day by day. We have to deal with new situations as they unfold and respond as best we can. Over time, particular situations will arise during this uncharted season which will require particular, concrete, Christ-like responses. *Why?* is a valid question, but so is *What?* What can *I* do in a practical way to make the best of this unfortunate situation? What can *we* do as members of a local church? And what can people of faith everywhere do to respond to this situation in ways that are Godly? What does this new and evolving 'moment' require of us?

In watching BBC News last night, I saw a British healthcare official saying to his nation: "This is your moment to act in ways that will actually save lives." A profound statement. This is *your* moment. There are things *you* can do that will save lives.

John 9:5: "As long as I am in the world, I am the light of the world." We know that Jesus is with us in Spirit. Today, the nave is almost empty of people. There are just a handful of us here, but we know that many others are with us 'in Spirit.' We know that even in the midst of social distancing we remain connected to each other in this local church, and to our sisters and brothers in Christ the world over. The Spirit, the light of Christ, is with us.

In commenting on our passage, N.T. Wright observes: "When surrounded by fear and anger, the only way through is to glimpse whatever we can see of Jesus, and to follow him out of the dark, and into the light."[1] Amen.

CHAPTER THREE
CHANGED EYES

Friday in the Fourth Week of Lent
27 March 2020 • John 9:1-41

¹ As he walked along, he saw a man blind from birth. ² His disciples asked him, "Rabbi, who sinned, this man or his parents, that he was born blind?" ³ Jesus answered, "Neither this man nor his parents sinned; he was born blind so that God's works might be revealed in him. ⁴ We must work the works of him who sent mewhile it is day; night is coming when no one can work. ⁵ As long as I am in the world, I am the light of the world." ⁶ When he had said this, he spat on the ground and made mud with the saliva and spread the mud on the man's eyes, ⁷ saying to him, "Go, wash in the pool of Siloam" (which means Sent). Then he went and washed and came back able to see. ⁸ The neighbors and those who had seen him before as a beggar began to ask, "Is this not the man who used to sit and beg?" ⁹ Some were saying, "It is he." Others were saying, "No, but it is someone like him." He kept saying, "I am the man." ¹⁰ But they kept asking him, "Then how were your eyes opened?" ¹¹ He answered, "The man called Jesus made mud,

spread it on my eyes, and said to me, 'Go to Siloam and wash.' Then I went and washed and received my sight." [12] They said to him, "Where is he?" He said, "I do not know." [13] They brought to the Pharisees the man who had formerly been blind. [14] Now it was a sabbath day when Jesus made the mud and opened his eyes. [15] Then the Pharisees also began to ask him how he had received his sight. He said to them, "He put mud on my eyes. Then I washed, and now I see." [16] Some of the Pharisees said, "This man is not from God, for he does not observe the sabbath." But others said, "How can a man who is a sinner perform such signs?" And they were divided. [17] So they said again to the blind man, "What do you say about him? It was your eyes he opened." He said, "He is a prophet." [18] The Jews did not believe that he had been blind and had received his sight until they called the parents of the man who had received his sight [19] and asked them, "Is this your son, who you say was born blind? How then does he now see?" [20] His parents answered, "We know that this is our son, and that he was born blind; [21] but we do not know how it is that now he sees, nor do we know who opened his eyes. Ask him; he is of age. He will speak for himself." [22] His parents said this because they were afraid of the Jews; for the Jews had already agreed that anyone who confessed Jesus to be the Messiah would be put out of the synagogue. [23] Therefore his parents said, "He is of age; ask him." [24] So for the second time they called the man who had been blind, and they said to him, "Give glory to God! We know that this man is a sinner." [25] He answered, "I do not know whether he is a sinner. One thing I do know, that though I was blind, now I see." [26] They said to him, "What did he do to you? How did he open your eyes?" [27] He answered them, "I have told you already, and you would not listen. Why do you want to hear it again? Do you also want to become his disciples?" [28] Then they reviled him, saying, "You are his disciple, but we are disciples of Moses. [29] We know that God has spoken to Moses, but as for this man, we do not know where he comes from." [30] The man answered, "Here is an astonishing thing! You do not know where he comes from, and yet he opened my eyes. [31] We know that God does not listen to sinners, but he does listen to one who worships him and obeys his will. [32] Never since the world began has it been heard that anyone opened the eyes of a person born blind. [33] If this man were not from God, he could do nothing." [34] They answered him, "You were born entirely in sins, and are you trying to teach us?" And they drove him out. [35] Jesus heard that they had driven him out, and when he found him, he said, "Do you believe in the Son of Man?" [36] He answered, "And who is he, sir? Tell me, so that I may believe in him." [37] Jesus said to him, "You have seen him, and the one speaking with you is he." [38] He said, "Lord, I believe." And he worshiped him. [39] Jesus said, "I came into this world for judgment so that those who do not see may see, and those who do see may become blind." [40] Some of the Pharisees near him heard this and said to him, "Surely we are not blind, are we?" [41] Jesus said to them, "If you were blind, you would not have sin. But now that you say, 'We see,' your sin remains."

John 9:2 reads: "His disciples asked him, 'Rabbi, who sinned, this man or his parents, that he was born blind?'" The disciples here are evincing a theology which held that the sins of ancestors could be visited upon their children. We see examples of this theology in Exodus 20:5; 34:7; Psalm 109:13-15; and Isaiah 65:6-7. Though the idea that children may pay for the sins of their ancestors can be found in Hebrew Scriptures, in Ezekiel 18 the prophet expressly rejects this theology. The question of whether the sins of ancestors are visited upon their descendants provides evidence that, even within canonical Scripture, theology tends to evolve over time. Be that as it may, Jesus' answer is clear in John 9:3a: "Neither this man nor his parents sinned..."

In verse 5 Jesus says: "As long as I am in the world, I am the light of the world." This statement picks up on a key theme from John 1. From the beginning of his Gospel, John frames Jesus in terms of light. Jesus is the light of the world; the darkness of the world cannot overcome the light of Christ. In his commentary on 9:5, N.T. Wright observes: "When surrounded by fear and anger, the only way through is to glimpse whatever we can see of Jesus, and to follow him out of the dark and into the light."[1] This is a particularly timely observation given where we are in this COVID-19 outbreak. When *surrounded* by fear and anger, the only way through is to glimpse whatever we can see of Jesus, and to follow him *out* of the dark and *into* the light.

Verses 6-7 deal with the healing event itself, the blind man receiving his sight, and then verses 8-12 deal with the reaction to this healing. In verses 13-15, a number of Pharisees criticize Jesus for offering healing on the Sabbath. These Pharisees attack Jesus' action in terms of their dedication to Jewish law which prohibits work on the Sabbath. John writes in verse 16: "Some of the Pharisees said, 'This man is not from God, for he does not observe the Sabbath.'" John then notes: "But others said, 'How can a man who is a sinner perform such signs?'" The passage cautions us regarding the danger of lumping people into one group and then assuming that membership in, or affiliation with, that group makes all in the group of one mind. We are always to deal with people in their individuality. John is quite clear—some of the Pharisees see Jesus' action as a violation of Sabbath law, but others of them see the power of God at work in Jesus. *How can a man who is a sinner perform such signs?*

Then verse 17: "So they said again to the blind man, 'What do you say about him? It was your eyes he opened.'" The man answers: "He is a prophet." Obviously, the man who has been healed has a radically different perspective than Jesus' critics! The man born blind *experiences*—he knows first-hand—Jesus' healing power. We are reminded here of the importance of perspective, of point of view. Everything that we think, consciously or unconsciously, is grounded in our perspectives, our experiences, and our filters. Taking into account perspective is crucial to us being able to have meaningful conversations with one another. It is imperative that we try to see, and to respect, other points of view.

The blind man's parents get involved in the narrative in verses 18-21, and we encounter John's habit of referring to "the Jews." Scholars think that this terminology reflects the historical context in which John's Gospel was written. Most scholars think that John is the latest of the four canonical Gospels, having been written ca. 90-100 AD. John's usage of "the Jews" probably reflects conflict in the local synagogue between Jewish Christians and others in the synagogue who do not see Jesus as Messiah. In our contemporary context so frequently characterized by divisiveness, we are well-advised to be careful regarding our understanding of John's usage of "the Jews" in order to avoid an unintended, unconscious anti-Semitism.

Verse 22 reads: "His parents said this because they were afraid of the Jews; for the Jews had already agreed that anyone who confessed Jesus to be the Messiah would be put out of the synagogue." Most scholars think that here the author reflects his own time and experience regarding synagogue life in the late first-century. It was a decidedly negative experience to be removed from the synagogue in John's time. A synagogue was not merely a place of worship and did not function simply as what we would call a church. The synagogue was the place of education in a community. It served as what we might call the 'community center.' It was the gathering place for a community. The prospect of being removed from the synagogue was life-altering.

Given their anxiety stemming from the possible termination of their own participation in the synagogue, the man's parents deflect the attention back onto their son. Jesus' critics say in verse 24: "Give glory to God! We know that this man is a sinner." The man replies: "I do not know whether he is a sinner. One thing I do know, that though I was blind, now I see." *Though I was blind, now I see* provides the foundational theology underlying one of the most beloved Christian hymns of all time, *Amazing Grace*.

In verse 28 we read: "Then they reviled him, saying, 'You are his disciple, but we are disciples of Moses.'" Here again we encounter the issue of Jesus and Messiahship. "We know that God has spoken to Moses, but as for this man, we do not know where he comes from (v. 29)." Here John gets to the crux of the matter. There are those in the faith community so grounded in tradition that they have trouble being open to something new. Think about the generations of Messianic expectation within Judaism. Generation after generation after generation had looked forward to the coming of Messiah. Jesus' actions can be seen as indicating that the waiting is over, and that the time has been fulfilled. The time is *now*, and yet there are those who, because of their dedication to tradition, are unable to see the 'new' that is right before their very eyes.

The dialogue continues in verses 32-34 with the healed man saying: "'Never since the world began has it been heard that anyone opened the eyes of a person born blind. If this man were not from God, he could do nothing.' They answered him, 'You were born entirely in sins, and are you trying to teach us?'" Here again we encounter the theological notion that children are liable for the sins of their ancestors. And here we see the real-world consequences of theological division. Jesus has shown the love of God in a tangible way, and yet the response of his critics is that he has violated Sabbath law, and thus his action, far from representing Messiahship, is in fact sinful.

In verses 35-41, John shifts the discourse away from physical blindness to spiritual blindness. Some of the Pharisees say in verse 40: "Surely we are not blind, are we?" They know that of which they are being accused. They are being challenged to contemplate the prospect that, though they are religious leaders, the elite of the local religious community, their spiritual blindness is keeping them from seeing the power of God at work.

The moment in history in which we find ourselves is providing us with an opportunity to ask ourselves: How is it that *we* see? *What* do we see? And, how might our sight, our 'vision,' evolve—both now and going forward? How does the pandemic, our current public health crisis, change our perspective? How might our horizons be broadened during this experience? How might we become more aware of others around us, particularly those who are most vulnerable? How do we respond in *this* moment to our new reality? Of course, a part of our response involves vision. What do we see happening? Do we see how it is impacting others? How do we see our own changing realities?

In their commentary on John, Gail O'Day and Susan E. Hylen write in summary of 9:1-41 about the man who has been healed: "His gift of sight has deepened from physical sight to include spiritual and theological sight."[2] The man's physical healing translates into broadened spiritual insight.

With the benefit of hindsight, it is easy to be critical of the subset of Pharisees in this narrative who protest Jesus' healing of a man who had been born blind. In hindsight, it is obvious to us that Jesus has done God's will. And yet, the narrative forces us to think about our own vision, our own *spiritual* sight. What does this passage have to teach us about having *our* eyes opened to the widest possible vision of the Spirit of God at work in the world? In commenting on our passage, Frances Taylor Gench notes: "...the church engages in ongoing discernment of the will and work of God in new times and places."[3] Her observation speaks directly to the moment in which we find ourselves: the church engages in *ongoing discernment* of the will and work of God *in new times and places.*

We find ourselves in a new time. Amidst a global pandemic, the world is in a new 'time and place.' How will the global Church respond? How do Christians the world over respond in this moment of crisis? How will we respond locally, both as individuals and as a parish church?

Again, John 9:25: "One thing I do know, that though I was blind, now I see." Gench notes of verse 25 that this man's experience of healing "...becomes a lens through which he thinks about the implications of his encounter with Jesus Christ."[4] Of course, this man's dramatic experience of healing shapes everything he thinks about who Jesus is. He is forever changed.

Where will this moment in time lead us spiritually? How will it transform us? Going forward, can we come to see the world with changed eyes? Amen.

CHAPTER FOUR

A SERVANT'S HEART

Palm Sunday
5 April 2020 • Matthew 21:1-11

[1] When they had come near Jerusalem and had reached Bethphage, at the Mount of Olives, Jesus sent two disciples, [2] saying to them, "Go into the village ahead of you, and immediately you will find a donkey tied, and a colt with her; untie them and bring them to me. [3] If anyone say anything to you, just say this, 'The Lord needs them.' And he will send them immediately." [4] This took place to fulfill what had been spoken through the prophet, saying, [5] "Tell the daughter of Zion, Look, your king is coming to you, humble, and mounted on a donkey, and on a colt, the foal of a donkey." [6] The disciples went and did as Jesus had directed them; [7] they brought the donkey and the colt, and put their cloaks on them, and he sat on them. [8] A very large crowd spread their cloaks on the road, and others cut branches from the trees and spread them on the road. [9] The crowds that went ahead of him and that followed were shouting, "Hosanna to the Son of David! Blessed is the one who comes in the name of the Lord! Hosanna in the highest heaven!" [10] When he

entered Jerusalem, the whole city was in turmoil, asking, "Who is this?" [11] The crowds were saying, "This is the prophet Jesus from Nazareth in Galilee."

In preparing for a sermon or a class, I typically use *The HarperCollins Study Bible*. Its section heading over Matthew 21:1-11 reads: "Jesus' Triumphal Entry into Jerusalem."[1] Leon Morris writes regarding Matthew 21:1-11: "The picture we get is one of great excitement."[2] *The New English Bible* translates verse 10: "When he entered Jerusalem the whole city went wild with excitement."

Just a note about historical context regarding this event. It was not live-streamed on Facebook! You could not watch the evening news to get a summary of what had happened. Nor could you wait until the next day and read about it in the newspaper. That said, let us try to imagine the growing excitement as Jesus entered the city. Imagine the crowds, a diverse cross-section of people all gathering to 'be there,' to be part of it all—to see, to hear. The questions before the crowds are: What is happening? And: Who is this?

The New Revised Standard Version of Matthew 21:10-11 reads: "When he entered Jerusalem, the whole city was in turmoil, asking, 'Who is this?' The crowds were saying, 'This is the prophet Jesus from Nazareth in Galilee.'" Again, 21:10 from *The New English Bible*: "When he entered Jerusalem the whole city went wild with excitement."

This was indeed a triumphal entry, and yet, Jesus chose to ride into Jerusalem on a donkey. Verse 5 is a blending of Zechariah 9:9 and Isaiah 62:11: "'Look, your King is coming to you, humble and mounted on a donkey...'" In his commentary on the passage, Craig L. Blomberg notes: "This Messiah comes in humility, gentleness, and peace."[3] Joe Kapolyo observes in *Africa Bible Commentary*: "The crowds in Jerusalem would probably have preferred the Messiah to be riding on a war horse."[4]

And in a summary statement, Donald A. Hagner notes in his commentary: "The irony was that the king, who really was the promised Messiah, came to Jerusalem not as a warrior upon a stallion but humbly as a servant—indeed, as the servant who had come to die."[5]

We read in 21:9: "'Hosanna to the Son of David! Blessed is the one who comes in the name of the Lord! Hosanna in the highest heaven!'" Just imagine the enthusiasm of the crowd in that cry of praise. We have here an allusion to Psalm 118:25-26. The Hebrew word *Hosanna* means "God save us." Scholars agree that by the time of Jesus it had become a general cry of praise. Again, just imagine the excitement—the energy, the enthusiasm, the joy—as a large crowd of people shout: *Hosanna to the Son of David! Blessed is the one who comes in the name of the Lord! Hosanna in the highest heaven!*

This *is* a triumphal entry. No doubt the crowd went wild with excitement. In reading Matthew 21:1-11, we have the benefit of 2,000 years of hindsight that the crowd did not have. While we have the benefit of *hindsight*, Jesus had the prophetic *insight* to know what was really happening on that first Palm Sunday. In his aforementioned comment, Hagner uses the word "irony." The irony of Palm Sunday is that Jesus would have known while riding into the city on a donkey, a symbol of humility, that his immediate future included betrayal, arrest, humiliation—the pain, the agony, the horror—of the cross. So there is great irony on Palm Sunday as the exuberantly joyful crowd celebrates without understanding what is in Jesus' immediate future.

Regarding my preaching and teaching, I am aware that I often say: "This is one of my favorite passages." Or I might say: "This is a particularly important passage." I do have a lot of favorite Bible passages, and a lot of them *are* particularly important in the grand sweep of the biblical narrative. As part of our Palm Sunday observance 2020, I would like to refer us to a passage in the Letter to the Hebrews. This really is one of the key passages in all the New Testament regarding a theological and practical understanding of Jesus. Hebrews 4:14-16:

> Since, then, we have a great high priest who has passed through the heavens, Jesus, the Son of God, let us hold fast to our confession. For we do not have a high priest who is unable to sympathize with our weaknesses, but we have one who in every respect has been tested as we are, yet without sin. Let us therefore approach the throne of grace with boldness, so that we may receive mercy and find grace to help in time of need.

This is truly one of the foundational passages in all the New Testament. Here we find stated clearly, succinctly, and profoundly, the theology of the incarnation.

There *was* a triumphal entry into the holy city on that first Palm Sunday. The crowd would have been overcome with excitement and joy. These are Messianic cries that come from the crowd: *Hosanna! Welcome to the son of David!* But in the midst of it all Jesus chooses a donkey to carry him into the city, not a war horse. Jesus made the connection to the Hebrew Scriptures. He would have known Zechariah. The donkey is a symbol of humility, a conscious choice freighted with meaning. As Jesus arrived in Jerusalem for what we call Holy Week, he arrived with a servant's heart. He arrived in humility. No doubt he knew, amidst the cheers of the crowd, that his immediate future would be pain and suffering—even death.

None of us, in our lifetimes, can remember a Holy Week that has begun under these circumstances. Today, and in the coming days as we reflect on this year's Holy Week, we are wise to interpret the events of Palm Sunday through the lens of Hebrews 4:14-16. We, in fact, do not have a high priest who is unable to sympathize with our weaknesses. Jesus chose a path of humility. He understands every human frailty, every human emotion. And what we are met with in him is not judgment, nor indifference, and certainly not incomprehension, but compassion. As we observe Palm Sunday may we do so remembering not only the triumphal entry, but also Jesus' spirit of humility. His choice of animal tells us everything about Jesus' mindset. He rode into Jerusalem with a servant's heart, and with a spirit of compassion. Today, may we remember his humility, and that his Spirit is with us even now—to comfort us on the one hand, and to strengthen us on the other—so that we face this unprecedented time in the Spirit of Christ, with humility and resolve. Amen.

CHAPTER FIVE
THE BONDS OF CHRISTIAN COMMUNITY

Maundy Thursday, 12:00pm
9 April 2020 • 1 Corinthians 11:23-26

[23] For I received from the Lord what I also handed on to you, that the Lord Jesus on the night when he was betrayed took a loaf of bread, [24] and when he had given thanks, he broke it and said, "This is my body that is for you. Do this in remembrance of me." [25] In the same way he took the cup also, after supper, saying, "This cup is the new covenant in my blood. Do this, as often as you drink it, in remembrance of me." [26] For as often as you eat this bread and drink the cup, you proclaim the Lord's death until he comes.

In April of 1997, I went to a conference on Anglican Spirituality at the Cathedral Church of the Advent, Birmingham, Alabama. "The Truth About Jesus" drew a large crowd and featured an A-list group of speakers, including N.T. Wright, Alister McGrath, and Fleming Rutledge, among others.

On the first night of the conference, when it came time for dinner, I looked around the banquet hall and it appeared to me that nearly every seat was taken, and the room appeared to be filled with extroverts! Everyone (except me) seemed to know everyone else. Eventually I spotted the lone unoccupied *table* and took a seat. I was only semi-comfortable in the solitude, sensing that everyone else seemed to know each other, and that I was, once again, 'odd man out' in another large gathering of seemingly wildly extroverted clergy: not unknown territory for me. All of that said, as I was beginning to eat I heard someone with a lovely English accent say: "May I join you?" I looked up from my plate and over my right shoulder to see Robert Runcie, who had only recently retired as Archbishop of Canterbury. In an instant, I went from odd man out to having a private audience with the 102nd Archbishop of Canterbury, one of the most recognizable Christian leaders in the world.

He and I had dinner together, one-on-one, for the entire time. It was wonderful. We had an engaging, wide-ranging conversation. A high point of the conversation occurred when I told him that I was from Chattanooga, and he replied: "Oh, I've been to Chattanooga. The House of Bishops met there a number of years ago, and I was the keynote speaker." He continued: "You know, I got a key to the city of Chattanooga and it is my favorite of all the keys to cities I've been given. The key to the city of Chattanooga has a corkscrew attached to it, and I actually use it." As dinner went on, I could hear people at the other tables whispering: "Who is that with the Archbishop?" "They must be friends." Of course, we had never met.

In looking back on that memorable evening, I can readily recall that early on I was on the outside looking in: a shy introvert who, once again, could not find a comfortable seat at the table. While certainly painless in the grand scheme of things, it was nonetheless uncomfortable in the moment. I felt left out. And then, in an instant, I was included—wonderfully included—thanks to a moment of graciousness from a servant of Christ. *May I join you?*

In 1 Corinthians 11:23-24, Paul writes: "For I received from the Lord what I also handed on to you, that the Lord Jesus on the night when he was betrayed took a loaf of bread, and when he had given thanks, he broke it and said, 'This is my body that is for you.'" I mentioned a moment ago that Fleming Rutledge was one of the speakers at the conference. In a collection of sermons titled, *The Undoing of Death*, Rutledge notes in a Maundy Thursday address: "This is family night."[1] What a great way to think about Maundy Thursday—*Family Night*. On Maundy Thursday, Family Night, we remember, we commemorate—we celebrate—the institution of the Eucharist. Rutledge's description of Maundy Thursday is insightful because the Eucharist is, in the end, a family meal. Of course, we are always meant to be widening the circle of those who constitute the family. Everyone is invited. All are meant to be welcomed to the family dinner we call Holy Eucharist.

Maundy Thursday—Family Night—'family' and friends gathered in the name of Christ. In the Gospel of John's description of that historic Thursday evening (15:15-16), we read: "[Jesus said] I do not call you servants any longer, because the servant does not know what the master is doing; but I have called you friends, because I have made known to you everything that I have heard from my Father. You did not choose me but I chose you." Here we have recorded for posterity a deeply intimate moment between Jesus and his disciples. *You did not choose me but I chose you.* Graciousness. Invitation. Family.

This year's Family Night will be different in this time of social distancing. In observing Maundy Thursday 2020, we have never known a Family Night quite like this one. And yet, we are still family. Returning to Fleming Rutledge, she observes that the love of Christ makes us "...brothers and sisters at the deepest level..."[2] What a beautiful description of Christian community: *brothers and sisters at the deepest level.* Social distancing cannot break the bonds of Christian community. Maundy

Thursday *is* different this year, but in this unusual circumstance we are reminded of the deep, unbreakable bonds that we share in the love of Christ.

Yesterday, Debbie and I had a moment with one of our dearest friends. Dixie lives in Chattanooga and could be my mother in terms of our age difference. During our brief visit with her, Dixie said to us: "This Easter will be different." Of course, we agreed. There was a moment's pause, and then she said: "I think we have a lot to learn from this." My response was simply: "You're right. We do."

We do have a lot to learn from what we are experiencing—globally, nationally, regionally, and locally, right down to our parish's life—lessons that can shape the rest of our lives. May this unusual, hopefully once-in-a-lifetime, experience of Maundy Thursday that includes social distancing, and limited in-person participation in Family Night, remind us in a meaningful way that, in the love of Christ, we are sisters and brothers at the deepest level, come what may. Amen.

CHAPTER SIX

THE VITAL IMPORTANCE OF CHRISTIAN COMMUNITY

Maundy Thursday, 6:00pm
9 April 2020 • John 13:1-17, 31b-35

[1] Now before the festival of the Passover, Jesus knew that his hour had come to depart from this world and go to the Father. Having loved his own who were in the world, he loved them to the end. [2] The devil had already put it into the heart of Judas son of Simon Iscariot to betray him. And during supper [3] Jesus, knowing that the Father had given all things into his hands, and that he had come from God and was going to God, [4] got up from the table, took off his outer robe, and tied a towel around himself. [5] Then he poured water into a basin and began to wash the disciples' feet and to wipe them with the towel that was tied around him. [6] He came to Simon Peter, who said to him, "Lord, are you going to wash my feet?" [7] Jesus answered, "You do not know now what I am doing, but later you will understand." [8] Peter said to him, "You will never wash my feet." Jesus answered, "Unless I wash you, you have no share with me." [9] Simon Peter said to him, "Lord, not my feet only but also my

hands and my head!" [10] Jesus said to him, "One who has bathed does not need to wash, except for the feet, but is entirely clean. And you are clean, though not all of you." [11] For he knew who was to betray him; for this reason he said, "Not all of you are clean."

[12] After he had washed their feet, had put on his robe, and had returned to the table, he said to them, "Do you know what I have done to you? [13] You call me Teacher and Lord—and you are right, for that is what I am. [14] So if I, your Lord and Teacher, have washed your feet, you also ought to wash one another's feet. [15] For I have set you an example, that you also should do as I have done to you. [16] Very truly, I tell you, servants are not greater than their master, nor are messengers greater than the one who sent them. [17] If you know these things, you are blessed if you do them. [31b] "Now the Son of Man has been glorified, and God has been glorified in him. [32] If God has been glorified in him, God will also glorify him in himself and will glorify him at once. [33] Little children, I am with you only a little longer. You will look for me; and as I said to the Jews so now I say to you, 'Where I am going, you cannot come.' [34] I give you a new commandment, that you love one another. Just as I have loved you, you also should love one another. [35] By this everyone will know that you are my disciples, if you have love for one another."

During my first year of seminary at Sewanee, I was scheduled to be the acolyte on Maundy Thursday. I was still quite young then, in my mid-twenties, still very shy, and I was more than a little nervous being in front of the entire seminary community on such a big occasion. As you can imagine, in a seminary setting Holy Week services are very well attended. The preacher that evening was John Booty, a former dean of the seminary, who by my time was serving as professor of Anglican Studies. John had been granted the title "Historiographer of the Episcopal Church" by the General Convention of the Episcopal Church, Convention's way of acknowledging that John was the Episcopal Church's premiere historian of Anglican Christianity. In my second year at Sewanee, I served as John Booty's research assistant, and during that time we developed a comfortable, relaxed relationship. But in my first year, I was in awe of the man. He was our premiere church historian: Church History being one of my favorite areas of study. Truth be told, on that Maundy Thursday evening I was actually a little star-struck by John Booty.

John preached an excellent sermon that night. As is the case with most sermons, even the really good ones, all these years later I cannot recall a single word that he said. What I do remember thirty years later is what happened following the sermon. When it came time for the foot-washing, much to my surprise John Booty looked me in the eye and said: "Joel, may I wash your feet?" This was thirty years ago, and yet I can remember it as if it happened yesterday. *Joel, may I wash your feet?* I was startled. I was incredulous. I felt unworthy. And I can remember thinking in the moment: This is backwards. I should be washing *your* feet.

In John 13:6-9 we read: "He came to Simon Peter, who said to him, 'Lord, are you going to wash my feet?' Jesus answered, 'You do not know now what I am doing, but later you will understand.' Peter said to him, 'You will never wash my feet.' Jesus answered, 'Unless I wash you, you have no share with me.' Simon Peter said to him, 'Lord, not my feet only but also my hands and my head!'" Peter was startled. He was incredulous. He felt unworthy. No doubt Peter was thinking: This is backwards. I should be washing *your* feet.

When it comes to foot-washing, many of us may think in terms of following the example of our Lord, and we *are* to follow his example of humility. We are to follow Jesus' example and have a servant's heart. But in thinking about foot-washing, if we put all of our emphasis on what we are to *do*, if that is where all of our focus is, we may run the risk of putting the cart before the horse. In a Maundy Thursday sermon, Michael Mayne observes: "...the origin, the pattern, and the constant motivation of our Christian journey has to be our willingness not simply to give but first to receive."[1] And Fleming Rutledge states in a Maundy Thursday sermon: "...brothers and sisters in the family of our Lord Jesus, before we start talking about the service we owe to one another, we need to enter more deeply into the meaning of the service that Jesus renders to us."[2] These observations by Mayne and Rutledge may put us in mind of 1 John 4:10: "In this is love, not that we loved God but that he loved us and sent his Son to be the atoning sacrifice for our sins."

On a more normal Maundy Thursday, right about now we would be having a foot-washing service. On a typical Maundy Thursday, just about fifteen feet from where I am standing, we would be washing feet, following Jesus' example. But this is, of course, anything but a normal Maundy Thursday. Though we are not able to gather in-person this year, we are united spiritually. The social distancing that we are right to practice for now can, ironically, lead us to recognize and embrace a deeper sense of our spiritual unity. Not being able to gather together in-person this year reminds us just how important we are to each other spiritually. This season of pandemic presses home to us the vital importance of Christian community. We have an unprecedented opportunity this year, given the unusual circumstances of this Maundy Thursday, to be reminded in a lastingly meaningful and transformative way of just how important we are to one another.

All of which puts me in mind of 1 Corinthians 12:12-13. Paul is writing about the *body of Christ* and the interdependence within the body, the interconnectedness of one Christian to another. Paul makes it quite clear in I Corinthians 12—and this year's observance of Maundy Thursday reminds us in no uncertain terms—that no member of the body of Christ can ever say to another member of the body of Christ: I have no need of you. Amen.

CHAPTER SEVEN
HAVING NEW EYES

Easter Sunday
12 April 2020 • John 20:1-18

[1] Early on the first day of the week, while it was still dark, Mary Magdalene came to the tomb and saw that the stone had been removed from the tomb. [2] So she ran and went to Simon Peter and the other disciple, the one whom Jesus loved, and said to them, "They have taken the Lord out of the tomb, and we do not know where they have laid him." [3] Then Peter and the other disciple set out and went toward the tomb. [4] The two were running together, but the other disciple outran Peter and reached the tomb first. [5] He bent down to look in and saw the linen wrappings lying there, but he did not go in. [6] Then Simon Peter came, following him, and went into the tomb. He saw the linen wrappings lying there, [7] and the cloth that had been on Jesus' head, not lying with the linen wrappings but rolled up in a place by itself. [8] Then the other disciple, who reached the tomb first, also went in, and he saw and believed; [9] for as yet they did not understand the scripture, that he must rise from the dead. [10] Then the disciples returned to their homes. [11] But

Mary stood weeping outside the tomb. As she wept, she bent over to look into the tomb; [12] and she saw two angels in white, sitting where the body of Jesus had been lying, one at the head and the other at the feet. [13] They said to her, "Woman, why are you weeping?" She said to them, "They have taken away my Lord, and I do not know where they have laid him." [14] When she had said this, she turned around and saw Jesus standing there, but she did not know that it was Jesus. [15] Jesus said to her, "Woman, why are you weeping? Whom are you looking for?" Supposing him to be the gardener, she said to him, "Sir, if you have carried him away, tell me where you have laid him, and I will take him away." [16] Jesus said to her, "Mary!" She turned and said to him in Hebrew, "Rabbouni!" (which means Teacher). [17] Jesus said to her, "Do not hold on to me, because I have not yet ascended to the Father. But go to my brothers and say to them, 'I am ascending to my Father and your Father, to my God and your God.'" [18] Mary Magdalene went and announced to the disciples, "I have seen the Lord"; and she told them that he had said these things to her.

I was in seminary at Sewanee from September, 1988, through May, 1990. During that time Sam Lloyd was University Chaplain. Sam went on from Sewanee to be Rector of Trinity Church, Copley Square, Boston. From there he continued on to be Dean of Washington National Cathedral. Then Sam went back to Trinity Church, Boston, again to serve as rector. During my time in seminary I got into the habit of going to All Saints' Chapel (the University Chapel) on Sunday mornings. More Sundays than not, Sam was the preacher. Sam has a PhD in literature, and frequently includes in his sermons a wide range of literary references. Although I was not conscious of it at the time, Sam Lloyd would have a lot to do with my formation as a priest, particularly in terms of preaching.

Sam's sermons were always outstanding, but there is one

sermon in particular that I remember all these years later. We seniors had just taken our General Ordination Exams after the Christmas break. GOEs for aspiring clergy in the Episcopal Church are akin to the bar exam that law students take after graduating law school. As you can imagine, it was not the most relaxed Christmas ever! GOEs are by their very nature anxiety-producing. Sam Lloyd was the preacher at the Eucharist which marked the end of our exam time. I certainly do not remember every word of the sermon, but I do remember the main point, which was: *You did your best. It's over now. Leave the results to God.* This was thirty years ago, and in my mind I can still remember the tone of Sam's voice. You did your best...leave the results to God. That sermon in early January, 1990, was spot on. It met the moment.

There is a collection of Sam Lloyd's sermons from his time as Dean of Washington National Cathedral, and in preparing for this year's celebration of Easter I read a couple of Sam's Easter sermons. In one of those Easter sermons he notes: "Easter demands that we reframe how we see the world."[1]

On that first Easter morning, Mary Magdalene went to the tomb to grieve. In real time she would have been heartbroken, devastated—inconsolable. We read the Easter narratives with the benefit of hindsight, with 2,000 years worth of Christian history and theological reflection in hand. When we read the Easter story, we know where it is heading! But in the moment, in real time, Mary Magdalene would have been devastated in the pre-dawn hours of that first Easter morning and in the depths of despair as she made her way in the darkness to the tomb.

John tells us: "Early on the first day of the week, while it was still dark..." We can only try to imagine the grief and pain that Mary Magdalene was experiencing. She went to the tomb to grieve over Jesus' corpse. But then came the moment when she encountered the risen Christ, and in that moment she became the apostle to the apostles. In 20:18 John tells us that Mary returned to find Jesus' friends and exclaimed: "I have seen the Lord..." For Christians the world over, these words mark the turning point of history.

Easter demands that we reframe how we see the world. To be sure, *this Easter is* different. When I was in seminary all those years ago and listening to Sam Lloyd on a regular basis, I could not have imagined a time when I would preach an Easter sermon in a room filled with pews left empty by design. As I watched the late evening news this past Friday, the anchor signed off from her broadcast with: "This Easter is going to be really weird."

Easter is different this year, and my message is, in the end, straightforward. This Easter really does demand that we reframe how we see the world. Sam Lloyd would approve of my bringing in a reference to the French novelist Marcel Proust, who once observed: "The real voyage of discovery consists not in seeing new landscapes, but in having new eyes."[2]

Our celebration of Easter in 2020 *is* different. We are out of our comfort zones. Our annual traditions are not playing out as normal this year. Easter 2020 is, in fact, *really weird.* And yet, rather than lamenting how different this year's Easter is, we can choose to meet the moment head on. Or, put another way, we can choose to allow this year's Easter observance to reframe how we see the world. Of all the Easters we have ever experienced, this year we really do face the challenge of seeing with new eyes.

One of the distinctives of the Gospel of John is its introduction, the Prologue. John 1:1-18 is a discrete section, a preamble that sets the table for the entire Gospel to come. In the Prologue, we get a remarkably revealing preview of where the remainder of the narrative will take us. In 1:5 John writes: "The light shines in the darkness, and the darkness did not overcome it." The light of Christ still shines, even amidst the darkness of 2020. The darkness did not—and will not—overcome it. The tomb is empty, and Christ *is* with us! Alleluia! Amen.

CHAPTER EIGHT

ONCE YOU LABEL ME, YOU NEGATE ME

Thursday in the Second Week of Easter
23 April 2020 • John 20:24-29

[24] But Thomas (who was called the Twin), one of the twelve, was not with them when Jesus came. [25] So the other disciples told him, "We have seen the Lord." But he said to them, "Unless I see the mark of the nails in his hands, and put my finger in the mark of the nails and my hand in his side, I will not believe." [26] A week later his disciples were again in the house, and Thomas was with them. Although the doors were shut, Jesus came and stood among them and said, "Peace be with you." [27] Then he said to Thomas, "Put your finger here and see my hands. Reach out your hand and put it in my side. Do not doubt but believe." [28] Thomas answered him, "My Lord and my God!" [29] Jesus said to him, "Have you believed because you have seen me? Blessed are those who have not seen and yet have come to believe."

Typically, every small town has at least one beloved educator whom 'everyone' can remember—someone who taught generations of students, and whom 'everyone' in town seems to have known. In my hometown that person is "Miss Amy" Smith. Miss Amy was teaching when my parents were in high school in the 1950s, and by the time my sister and I came along she was still going strong. Amy Smith spent her entire adult life in the service of public education. When a student would have a moment of insight, Miss Amy would lift her index finger and exclaim: "Raise the flag!" In my mind, I can hear it as if she were saying it right now: *Raise the flag!* On the other hand, when we were struggling, when we were not 'getting it,' Miss Amy would say: "Don't be a doubting Thomas." I am fifty-seven years old, yet in my mind I can still hear Miss Amy encouraging us: *Don't be a doubting Thomas.*

History is filled with the names of people who made their mark in *one* moment. It can have been a moment of triumph. Before his heroic landing on the Hudson, who had ever heard of Captain Chesley Sullenberger? Of course, his family, friends, and colleagues. But on a national level we did not know "Sully" until that day when he saved 155 lives by drawing on his years of training, his vast experience, his calmness under pressure, and his sheer courage. Overnight, Sully became a national hero, and rightly so.

Bill Buckner made an error in the 1986 World Series that cost the Boston Red Sox a game and, ultimately, the Series to the New York Mets. More than three decades on, if you Google "Bill Buckner," the first thing that comes up is: "Bill Buckner Error." Bill Buckner had a Hall of Fame caliber career: over 2,700 base hits, over 1,200 runs batted in, and a .280+ career batting average. These are Hall of Fame-like numbers, career statistics arguably worthy of Cooperstown. But, what we most remember about "Billy Buck" is that one moment, in that one game, when a likely Hall of Famer had *one* moment of failure.

History remembers people either for their moment of triumph or for a moment when they were not at their best. For reasons unknown to us, Thomas was not there that day when the risen Christ first appeared to his disciples. Over the years, there has been speculation by scholars that perhaps Thomas was so grief-stricken that he just could not bear to be with his friends on that first Sunday after the crucifixion. This is only speculation. We seemingly cannot resist theorizing about why Thomas was not there. Perhaps it *was* his grief that kept him away. Or he may have stepped out for a loaf of bread and a gallon of milk! We simply do not know *why*, but we do know *that* he missed the moment; he was not present when the risen Christ first appeared to his inner circle. But everything else we know about Thomas indicates that he was a loyal, faithful disciple. He was loyal and faithful before that one moment, and he went on to be loyal and faithful afterwards as well.

A week later, Thomas *was* present, and he saw with his own eyes. Jesus says, in effect, *You can touch me. Go ahead, touch me* (Jn 20:27). The author of John subtly indicates, however, that Thomas does not need to touch. He sees, and responds: "My Lord and my God!"

So the moment for which history *could* remember Thomas is not his moment of doubt, but the moment when he has the insight and the courage to be the first of the disciples to explicitly acknowledge Jesus' divinity—My Lord *and* my God. *Doubting Thomas* could just as easily (and much more fairly) be remembered as Faithful Thomas if we just changed our perspective. Which moment do we choose to emphasize? That one, brief moment of doubt? *Or* his shining moment of faith? The latter seems to be much more indicative of who Thomas truly was: a loyal, faithful disciple.

In the mid-1980's, when I was a student at Candler School of

Theology, Emory University, I took several courses on nine-teenth-century European theology and spirituality. In those courses I encountered the writings of Søren Kierkegaard (1813-55), the Danish philosopher and theologian. What sticks in my mind most from all of that reading back in those days is one particular line from Kierkegaard: "Once you label me, you negate me." This is an extraordinary insight. *Once you label me, you negate me.* Kierkegaard's concern is that once we place someone in a category, a grouping—once we assign an adjective or a label—they then become to us that category or that label instead of an *individual* human being made in the image and likeness of God. Kierkegaard offers us a lastingly instructive insight which has everything to do with our lives in the here and now given the divisive rhetoric, the hyperpartisanship, the 'cancel culture' with which we have become so familiar. *Once you label me, you negate me.*

We so often instinctively think in binary terms: you (or they) are either 'with us' or 'against us.' Consciously or uncon-sciously, we tend to place others in *this* or *that* category. The danger of such binary thinking is that we lose sight of the indi-vidual, and the unique space that each one of us has been given —uniquely and irreplaceably created in the image of God. *Once you label me, you negate me.* Once you place me in a category, in a 'box,' you miss *me* in my God-given uniqueness.

For 2,000 years we have remembered *Doubting Thomas* when —with just a small shift in perspective—we could just as well remember *Faithful Thomas,* or even *Courageous Thomas.* By chapter 11 of John's narrative, Jesus has sparked fierce opposition from his most ardent critics in Bethany of Judea, yet he proposes that he and the disciples return there to minister to Mary, Martha, and Lazarus. The disciples demur (11:8), citing the dangers of returning in the face of such hostile opposition. Only Thomas responds courageously: "Let us also go, that we may die with him (11:16)."

Once you label me, you negate me. We are unwise to place individuals, or whole groups of people, into a 'box,' assigning a category to them without actually knowing them or their situation: without thinking of them in a broader context. We really could just as easily think in terms of *Faithful Thomas*, or *Courageous Thomas*. We could, and probably should.

The case of Thomas reminds us that, almost always, we are much better advised to be slow to judge, and quick to listen. Amen.

CHAPTER NINE

WHAT MATTERS MOST

Third Sunday of Easter
26 April 2020 • Luke 24:13-35

[13] Now on that same day two of them were going to a village called Emmaus, about seven miles from Jerusalem, [14] and talking with each other about all these things that had happened. [15] While they were talking and discussing, Jesus himself came near and went with them, [16] but their eyes were kept from recognizing him. [17] And he said to them, "What are you discussing with each other while you walk along?" They stood still, looking sad. [18] Then one of them, whose name was Cleopas, answered him, "Are you the only stranger in Jerusalem who does not know the things that have taken place there in these days?" [19] He asked them, "What things?" They replied, "The things about Jesus of Nazareth, who was a prophet mighty in deed and word before God and all the people, [20] and how our chief priests and leaders handed him over to be condemned to death and crucified him. [21] But we had hoped that he was the one to redeem Israel. Yes, and besides all this, it is now the third day since these things took place. [22] Moreover, some

women of our group astounded us. They were at the tomb early this morning, [23] and when they did not find his body there, they came back and told us that they had indeed seen a vision of angels who said that he was alive. [24] Some of those who were with us went to the tomb and found it just as the women had said; but they did not see him." [25] Then he said to them, "Oh, how foolish you are, and how slow of heart to believe all that the prophets have declared! [26] Was it not necessary that the Messiah should suffer these things and then enter into his glory?" [27] Then beginning with Moses and all the prophets, he interpreted to them the things about himself in all the scriptures. [28] As they came near the village to which they were going, he walked ahead as if he were going on. [29] But they urged him strongly, saying, "Stay with us, because it is almost evening and the day is now nearly over." So he went in to stay with them. [30] When he was at the table with them, he took bread, blessed and broke it, and gave it to them. [31] Then their eyes were opened, and they recognized him; and he vanished from their sight. [32] They said to each other, "Were not our hearts burning within us while he was talking to us on the road, while he was opening the scriptures to us?" [33] That same hour they got up and returned to Jerusalem; and they found the eleven and their companions gathered together. [34] They were saying, "The Lord has risen indeed, and he has appeared to Simon!" [35] They then told what had happened on the road, and how he had been made known to them in the breaking of the bread.

One need not be a serious football fan to know the term 'Monday morning quarterback.' By Monday morning, what took place in the game over the weekend is clearer. By Monday morning, we know what the coach or a player *should* have done. By Monday morning, we have perspective on what happened. Everything is clearer by Monday morning than it was in the moment. Of course, in the end, the term 'Monday morning quarterback' is a reference to hindsight.

The precise definition of hindsight reads: "...perception of the nature and demands of an event after it has happened..."[1] And thus we have the expression: "Hindsight is 20/20." With the benefit of hindsight, we have a clearer perception of what happened, and what should have been done in real-time, and, in certain circumstances, what remains to be done.

Scholars agree that Luke is a consummate storyteller, a true literary artist. We see this in the Parable of the Good Samaritan in chapter 10, and in the Parable of the Prodigal Son in chapter 15. We see Luke's artistry in the much briefer Parable of the Pharisee and the Tax Collector in chapter 18. And, to be sure, we see Luke's literary skill on full display in the Walk to Emmaus. Some scholars go so far as to consider 24:13-35 to be Luke's masterpiece.

We read in verse 21: "But we had hoped that he was the one to redeem Israel." The verse can also be translated: "But we had hoped that he was the one to set Israel free." Frederick Buechner, in his book *Secrets in the Dark: A Life in Sermons*, notes regarding verse 21 that it includes: "...words as full of pathos as any in the New Testament."[2] The word "pathos" comes from the Greek meaning "to suffer." Pathos refers to a deep, emotional experience. Buechner continues: "'We had hoped that he was the one to redeem Israel,' they said, but by then their hope was as dead as they believed he was himself."[3]

In commenting on verse 21, David P. Moessner notes that what Luke is conveying is the "shattered hope" of these followers of Jesus.[4] Strong language: *shattered* hope.

What we are dealing with in Luke's beautifully told story is the real-time response of the followers of Jesus to his death, their response 'in the moment,' lacking, through no fault of their own, the perspective that we have when we read the story with two millennia worth of hindsight. On their walk home to

Emmaus in real time, without the benefit of hindsight, these two followers of Jesus are heartbroken. They are gutted. Everything they had hoped for and believed in is suddenly finished —shattered.

But as we read on, we come to verse 31: "Then their eyes were opened, and they recognized him..." Here is the rebirth of hope. Everything that these followers thought to be lost can now be restored. The Walk to Emmaus begins in 'darkness,' pain, and grief, but it ends in light, in the hope of restoration—a mysterious, bewildering, joyful hope. In this Easter season some 2,000 years later we proclaim the same good news, the same hope that these followers experienced in real-time on that first Easter Day: Christ is risen!

Luke is, in fact, a consummate literary artist. In our own time, Frederick Buechner is recognized as one of our great spiritual writers. In his summary comment on the Walk to Emmaus, Buechner states: "How extraordinary to have eyes...eyes that look out at this world we live in but, more often than not, see everything except what matters most."[5] Here Buechner is referring specifically to verse 31: *Then their eyes were opened, and they recognized him...* How extraordinary indeed to have eyes, eyes that look out at this world we have been given, more often than not seeing everything except *what matters most.*

Watching the news this past week about the COVID-19 outbreak, a reporter referred to 9/11 and employed the phrase: "eighteen years ago." It has been eighteen years since that unforgettably tragic day. In some ways, it seems like yesterday. It was *eighteen years ago,* and yet it feels like yesterday—the memories remain so fresh, so visceral. Like some other days in our history, it is said that anyone who lived through 9/11 can remember exactly where they were when they heard the news, and I can say that this is true of myself. On that fateful morning, I was in the process of leaving to go to work at St. Paul's Church, Chattanooga. I was literally in the process of walking toward the television to turn it off as the news was breaking. It just so happened that I did not have any early appointments that morning, and so I called the church secretary and said: "Something big is happening. I'm going to stay here for a while and watch the news." Eighteen years on, and I can still remember my exact words, my first verbal response to 9/11. And all these years later, I retain a lasting memory of my first emotional response: a visceral wave of outrage over the enormity of the crime, and the loss of so many innocent lives. We experienced that moment in real time, without any historical perspective, without the benefit of hindsight. In the moment we did not know exactly what it was, or when it would end, or how it would end.

Like 9/11, we are in the midst of another defining experience. Early on in the pandemic, I was talking by phone with someone who had a positive diagnosis and pronounced symptoms. I could hear her relentless, dry cough. I could hear her struggling for air. At one point she said: "It's just so hard to breathe." I can remember in that moment thinking: *This could be me. This could be Debbie. This could be anyone.*

For those of us in this local area, the tornadoes of Easter Sunday night have served to further intensify what we are experiencing in real-time. Having experienced life-threatening tornadoes on Easter night and their aftermath just adds to the seriousness of this moment in time. For all of us who came through the tornadoes unhurt, and our property largely intact, we have neighbors in this city and in our immediate region who are heartbroken, and whose disorientation and grief at least call to mind the two followers of Jesus on their walk home to Emmaus *before* their eyes were opened.

This is a defining moment for all of us, a time none of us will ever forget. We will remember this season for the rest of our lives, and, to be sure, it is bringing out the very best in many people. Every day we see quiet, or not so quiet, acts of kindness and compassion. Every day we see selflessness, and in some cases acts of extraordinary love and courage. Every day we see the best being brought out in some people. But, to be sure, we are seeing the worst as well. There is a terrible spike in violence, including domestic violence, here locally, as well as nationally. We are seeing the best and the worst of human nature in this intense time, and the seriousness of the moment causes us all to remember the seriousness of our calling to know and to make known the love of the risen Christ. On this, the Third Sunday of Easter, on 'Emmaus Sunday,' we remember and celebrate the moment those two heartbroken followers of Jesus had their eyes opened. In that moment, gut-wrenching loss was turned into victory, and despair began to give way to hope.

Then their eyes were opened, and they recognized him. This Third Sunday of Easter 2020 is a time for us to draw near to the risen Christ and his love as never before, and to remember what matters most. Amen.

CHAPTER TEN

THE PRISON OF MY OWN CREATION

24 May 2020 • 1 Peter 4:12-14; 5:6-11

^{12} Beloved, do not be surprised at the fiery ordeal that is taking place among you to test you, as though something strange were happening to you. ^{13} But rejoice insofar as you are sharing Christ's sufferings, so that you may also be glad and shout for joy when his glory is revealed. ^{14} If you are reviled for the name of Christ, you are blessed, because the spirit of glory, which is the Spirit of God, is resting on you. ^{6} Humble yourselves therefore under the mighty hand of God, so that he may exalt you in due time. ^{7} Cast all your anxiety on him, because he cares for you. ^{8} Discipline yourselves, keep alert. Like a roaring lion your adversary the devil prowls around, looking for someone to devour. ^{9} Resist him, steadfast in your faith, for you know that your brothers and sisters in all the world are undergoing the same kinds of suffering. ^{10} And after you have suffered for a little while, the God of all grace, who has called you to his eternal glory in Christ, will himself restore, support, strengthen, and establish you. ^{11} To him be the power forever and ever. Amen.

Every Bible reference book that I know of agrees that in the Bible there are 366 verses that say in one way or another: Do not fear, do not worry excessively—366— one for every day of the year including leap year. In the Gospels, Jesus addresses the pitfalls of excessive worry or fear. The best example is Matthew 6:25-34, where in verse 27, Jesus says: "And can any of you by worrying add a single hour to your span of life?" *Do not be afraid* is a biblical admonition, and in many cases it is exactly the right idea. But how realistic is it as a guiding principle for *all* times and situations? Can we really be expected to live without any fear?

Earlier in my career, when I was at St. Paul's, Chattanooga, for many months on my route home there sat a blue SUV parked on the street near where Barton Avenue becomes Hixson Pike. I saw this SUV nearly every day for months. Early on I noticed a bumper sticker on the back of the SUV that read: "Relax—God is in control." So nearly every day for months I looked at that bumper sticker and found it comforting, reassuring: *Relax—God is in control*. Until the day I saw that the rear end of that SUV had been smashed to smithereens.

As people of faith, we are not meant to be paralyzed by fear. But fear is an understandable, indeed an inevitable emotion in certain circumstances. Fear, worry, and anxiety are a part of being human. It is simply axiomatic that different times, situations, and challenges will evoke varying levels of fear, worry, or anxiety.

It is imperative for us to be careful in how we use words. One way to define fear is: "an unpleasant often strong emotion caused by anticipation or awareness of danger."[1] I can tell you that this past Easter night, when tornadoes were touching down all around us, I was afraid. Debbie and I stayed calm, we followed our emergency plan, and when the threat was finally over we each took a deep breath, offered prayers of thanksgiving, and then—at 3:00 a.m.—started sweeping out our flooded crawlspace! But as the tornadoes were hitting all around I was afraid for *us* and I was afraid for *you*.

Fear is a natural response to an identifiable danger. I am afraid of COVID-19. I have asthma, which, thankfully, is typically well controlled—until I get bronchitis, or the flu, or pneumonia. My normally robust health notwithstanding, I am at risk regarding COVID. I *am* afraid of COVID-19. But that said, we get on with living. We make prudent decisions. We take the necessary precautions. We follow the best advice of the medical community. COVID-19 is an identifiable danger. It is a real threat, and to be afraid of it for ourselves and for others is perfectly natural. Fear can serve as a mechanism by which we protect ourselves.

But then there is excessive, needless, utterly fruitless worry. Excessive worry is different from justifiable fear. One way to define needless anxiety is: a response to an *unidentified* threat or an *anticipated* danger. 'What if...' thinking typifies excessive worry. 'What if...': though the 'if' has yet to materialize.

We are wise to be careful in using words like *fear*, *worry*, or *anxiety*, especially in issuing too-easy prohibitions against these emotions. The words can have nuanced meanings in widely varying circumstances. What appears to be an illusory fear to one person can be quite real to another.

I have just finished reading a book by the best-selling author Cassandra King Conroy, who has written a memoir in the aftermath of her husband's death titled, *Tell Me A Story: My Life with Pat Conroy*. It is a compelling read. In the book, Cassandra King Conroy writes about her own years-long battle with excessive worry and anxiety, and how writing has been therapeutic. In fact, she became a writer in part as a means of coping with her anxiety. She saw writing as an outlet for her persistent, excessive worry. She notes in the book: "Through writing I finally was freed of that prison of my own creation, the deadly urge to please others, to let what others think of me become more important than what I think of myself."[2] What a profound way to frame the subject of excessive worry: it is like living in a prison of our own creation. Self-generated anxiety brings with it the *deadly urge* to please others, and to allow what others think of us to be more important than what we think of ourselves.

Some of us can relate to this passage from Cassandra King Conroy. You notice that I say *us* and not *you*. The English priest and spiritual writer Michael Mayne insightfully observed that people who write books, and people who preach sermons, oftentimes do so because of what they *lack*, not because of what they *have*. People who put themselves 'out there' frequently do so because of what they *lack*, not because of what they *have*. Here I am reminded of the truism: We teach what we want to learn.

I was well into my 30s when I finally addressed the prison of *my own* creation that I had been living in for years. I had been serving as an ordained minister for a decade when I finally looked squarely at the issue of anxiety in my own life. I will never forget my first visit with the psychologist who would become my therapist. He was a mature man, old enough to have been my grandfather, and when we settled in to talk for the first time I said to him: "Given what I do for a living, I'm a little embarrassed to be here. But I need help." He responded knowingly, graciously, and reassuringly. Then to get the conversation started in earnest he said: "Let me ask you a question. Are you a perfectionist?" My response: "I don't think so." Which produced a knowing smile on his kindly face, and then: "Well, let's talk about that." Which then led to the most productive fifteen weeks of my life, during which I finally named and addressed the excessive worry, the anxiety, the *deadly urge* to please others which had ruled my entire life. It was a fruitful fifteen weeks of sometimes painful yet ultimately healing self-assessment which, over time, has turned my life around. It was the most rewarding, transformative fifteen weeks of my life, and I remain grateful for that difficult, yet life-changing, time of vulnerability and, ultimately, healing.

During my time in therapy, that season of transformation, a verse of Scripture became vitally important to me—1 Peter 5:7: "Cast all your anxiety on him, because he cares for you." Though a serious student of the Bible, somehow I had never really noticed this verse, or at least had never been affected by it. It is one of the great, haunting verses in all of Scripture: *Cast all your anxiety on him, because he cares for you*. The Greek verb typically translated here as "cast" can be translated as "hurl." "Hurl all your anxiety on him, because he cares for you." The Common English Bible translates it: "Throw all your anxiety onto him, because he cares about you." And The New Jerusalem Bible has: "...unload all your burden on to him, since he is concerned about you." All of which builds on an insight from Psalm 55:22: "Cast your burden on the LORD, and he will sustain you..."

A certain level of fear is, on occasion, simply a part of life and is perfectly natural, indeed inevitable, in certain situations. Fear can be a means of self-preservation in the presence of an identifiable danger. There are moments when we *ought* to be fearful of a real threat. And yet we are to be vigilant regarding excessive worry, needless anxiety over things we simply cannot control. We are wise to take a pass on anxiety over things that have not yet happened and might not happen: *What if...* thinking. In building on wisdom from the Hebrew Scriptures, Jesus, and in his turn the author of 1 Peter, both caution: Do not let excessive, needless fear or anxiety—a prison of your own making—overwhelm you.

Matthew 6:27: "And can any of you by worrying add a single hour to your span of life?" Jesus' words here come from a place of deep, profoundly compassionate love: Can any of you, by worrying, add a *single hour* to your span of life? And then a little later on, in Matthew 11:28-30, Jesus says: "Come to me, all you that are weary and are carrying heavy burdens, and I will give you rest. Take my yoke upon you, and learn from me; for I am gentle and humble in heart, and you will find rest for your souls. For my yoke is easy, and my burden is light." Amen.

CHAPTER ELEVEN

THE SINGLE GARMENT OF DESTINY

Pentecost Sunday
31 May 2020 • Acts 2:1-21

[1] When the day of Pentecost had come, they were all together in one place. [2] And suddenly from heaven there came a sound like the rush of a violent wind, and it filled the entire house where they were sitting. [3] Divided tongues, as of fire, appeared among them, and a tongue rested on each of them. [4] All of them were filled with the Holy Spirit and began to speak in other languages, as the Spirit gave them ability. [5] Now there were devout Jews from every nation under heaven living in Jerusalem. [6] And at this sound the crowd gathered and was bewildered, because each one heard them speaking in the native language of each. [7] Amazed and astonished, they asked, "Are not all these who are speaking Galileans? [8] And how is it that we hear, each of us, in our own native language? [9] Parthians, Medes, Elamites, and residents of Mesopotamia, Judea and Cappadocia, Pontus and Asia, [10] Phrygia and Pamphylia, Egypt and the parts of Libya belonging to Cyrene, and visitors from Rome, both Jews and proselytes, [11] Cretans and Arabs—in our

own languages we hear them speaking about God's deeds of power." ¹² All were amazed and perplexed, saying to one another, "What does this mean?" ¹³ But others sneered and said, "They are filled with new wine."

¹⁴ But Peter, standing with the eleven, raised his voice and addressed them, "Men of Judea and all who live in Jerusalem, let this be known to you, and listen to what I say. ¹⁵ Indeed, these are not drunk, as you suppose, for it is only nine o'clock in the morning. ¹⁶ No, this is what was spoken through the prophet Joel:

¹⁷ 'In the last days it will be, God declares, that I will pour out my Spirit upon all flesh, and your sons and your daughters shall prophesy, and your young men shall see visions, and your old men shall dream dreams. ¹⁸ Even upon my slaves, both men and women, in those days I will pour out my Spirit; and they shall prophesy. ¹⁹ And I will show portents in the heaven above and signs on the earth below, blood, and fire, and smoky mist. ²⁰ The sun shall be turned to darkness and the moon to blood, before the coming of the Lord's great and glorious day. ²¹ Then everyone who calls on the name of the Lord shall be saved.'"

From his time as Dean of Washington National Cathedral, Sam Lloyd tells the story in a Pentecost sermon of an eighteenth-century tomb outside of Winchester, England. The tomb is that of the Countess of Huntington, and the inscription on the tomb reads: "She was a just, godly, righteous and sober lady, a firm believer in the Gospel of our Lord and Savior Jesus Christ, and devoid of the taint of enthusiasm."¹ Perfect for Pentecost Sunday in the Episcopal Church. Lloyd goes on to note in that sermon: "Order is in the Episcopal DNA."²

A number of years ago I was at a service in Westminster Cathedral in London. Not Westminster Abbey, but Westminster *Cathedral*, the Roman Catholic cathedral on Victoria Street. The service was Evensong, and in the middle of the service a man got up and quietly walked toward the crossing in the church, toward the altar, and once in the crossing, this man got down on the floor and lay prostrate in front of the altar for the remainder of the service. Keep in mind that this was in the Roman Catholic cathedral in London. In witnessing the man's actions, I thought to myself: If this were Westminster *Abbey,* instead of Westminster Cathedral, security would come and escort him out. Order *is* in the Episcopal DNA.

So here we are on Pentecost Sunday. Most of us know the term "C and E Christian." I do not particularly care for the term and try not to use it very often, but it is a term most of us know. A "C and E Christian" is someone who comes to church on Christmas and Easter, the two biggest feasts of the Christian year. Well, I think there are *three* 'biggest' feasts: Christmas and Easter, yes, but also Pentecost—C and E and P.

We think of Pentecost as the birthday of the Church, and that is right as far as it goes. But it is important on Pentecost Sunday not to think only in terms of history—the *Day* of Pentecost. On Pentecost Sunday we do not just look back. Pentecost Sunday is not merely a commemoration of that first Day of Pentecost.

Mark Oakley is one of the leading preachers in the Church of England. In a Pentecost sermon included in his book, *By Way of the Heart: The Seasons of Faith,* Mark Oakley states: "Pentecost is not like a birthday when we look back. Pentecost is the celebration of the future, a reminder that no matter how much we in the Church like to think we are doing the Spirit's work, actually, God's Spirit is always ahead of the Church, always before us, willing us to catch up, and that sometimes the Spirit has to show its work outside the Church so that Christians can be convinced they need to get moving."[3]

One of my favorite spiritual writers is Frederick Buechner. The title of one of Buechner's memoirs is, *Now and Then: A*

Memoir of Vocation. Great phrasing, Now *and* Then. On Pentecost Sunday, it is important for us to think both in terms of then *and* now. To observe Pentecost Sunday is not merely to look back, but to look to the present, and to look ahead.

This service is being livestreamed from St. Luke's Episcopal Church in Cleveland, Tennessee, "The City with Spirit." A number of years ago our civic leaders chose that moniker for this city—*The City with Spirit.* It can safely be said that no other community in the United States thinks and talks more about Pentecost, and Pentecostalism, than Cleveland, Tennessee. Every organization must know its neighborhood. Think about how many advertisements we see saying: "Your Hometown Bank," or "Your Hometown Realtor." A restaurant in Haywood County, North Carolina, where I used to live, has as its tag line: "Where the home folks eat."

It is important for a parish church to know its neighborhood. Over time, St. Luke's has an increasingly fruitful relationship with Lee University. Recently, just before the lockdown and social distancing, we wrapped up our Episcopal Teaching Series for the year called "Walk in Love, Part II." On every other Tuesday night during the series a group of young adults would meet afterwards and have conversation with each other, and though not all, most of these young adults are students at Lee University and grew up in a Pentecostal setting. In one of those Tuesday night discussions the subject of the Spirit came up, and one of the members of the group said about St. Luke's: "There is a quiet Pentecostalism here." A *quiet* Pentecostalism. A keen insight. What that young man was saying is that the Spirit *is* here. Pentecostals who are drawn to Anglican liturgy realize that they are not leaving the Spirit behind in coming to the Episcopal Church. There is a *quiet* Pentecostalism here, but it *is* here.

At a meeting around the same time, a long-time member of this church, someone who has for decades been at the center of this parish's life, said: "We're on fire." Which reminds us of

Acts 2:3: "Divided tongues, as of fire, appeared among them, and a tongue rested on each of them."

Mark Oakley notes in his aforementioned Pentecost sermon: "...when the Holy Spirit is at work it provokes very different reactions."[4] He goes on to say: "St. Paul told us how the Spirit flowers in us: love, joy, peace, patience, kindness, goodness, faithfulness, gentleness, self-control."[5] The fruit of the Spirit (Galatians 5:22-23).

On Pentecost Sunday 2020, we do commemorate the 'birthday' of the Church. In doing so, it is important to remember that the outpouring of the Spirit, both then and now, is communal. It is not so much that individual people are 'in the Spirit.' The Spirit is poured out on us all. Acts 2:1-4: "When the day of Pentecost had come, they were all together in one place. And suddenly from heaven there came a sound like the rush of a violent wind, and it filled the entire house where they were sitting. Divided tongues, as of fire, appeared among them, and a tongue rested on each of them. All of them were filled with the Holy Spirit and began to speak in other languages, as the Spirit gave them ability." Pentecost was, and is, a communal event. There is a book written by Matthias Wenk titled, *Community-Forming Power: The Socio-Ethical Role of the Spirit in Luke—Acts.* Notice the title: Community-Forming Power.

Modern-day Pentecostalism traces its roots to the Azusa Street Revival, which broke out in 1906 and lasted until 1915. The Azusa Street Revival refers to Azusa Street in Los Angeles, California. There is an Azusa Street in Cleveland, Tennessee, an homage to Azusa Street in Los Angeles. Writing about the Azusa Street revival, Selina Stone and Sherman Fletcher observe: "The Holy Spirit's action converted individuals, formed a *church* (emphasis mine) whose *common* (emphasis mine) life ran counter to the racial and social segregation of the day, and challenged structural injustice in the wider society."[6] The communal gift of the Spirit leads to prophetic vision—and action.

Jon Meacham wrote the foreword to the aforereferenced collection of sermons from the National Cathedral by Sam Lloyd. Jon Meacham is one of our great public historians, and has deep roots in this region. Meacham notes in his foreword that the last Sunday sermon preached by Dr. Martin Luther King, Jr., occurred in Washington National Cathedral on March 31, 1968. Dr. King's last Sunday sermon was given in the pulpit of an Episcopal church. In his last Sunday sermon, in 1968, from an Episcopal pulpit, Dr. King preached: "We are tied together in the single garment of destiny, caught in an inescapable network of mutuality... And whatever affects one directly affects all indirectly. For some strange reason, I can never be what I ought to be until you are what you ought to be. And you can never be what you ought to be until I am what I ought to be. This is the way God's universe is made; this is the way it is structured."[7]

One of the great hymns of the Church comes to us from the ninth century. The text of the hymn comes from the Latin, *Veni Creator Spiritus*. The first line of this ancient Christian hymn is: "Come Holy Ghost, our souls inspire, and lighten with celestial fire." Amen.

CHAPTER TWELVE

THE PORTRAIT OF GOD WE CALL THE TRINITY

Trinity Sunday
7 June 2020 • Matthew 28:16-20

[16] Now the eleven disciples went to Galilee, to the mountain to which Jesus had directed them. [17] When they saw him, they worshiped him; but some doubted. [18] And Jesus came and said to them, "All authority in heaven and on earth has been given to me. [19] Go therefore and make disciples of all nation, baptizing them in the name of the Father and of the Son and of the Holy Spirit, [20] and teaching them to obey everything that I have commanded you. And remember, I am with you always, to the end of the age."

I found the Episcopal Church in increments in my early 20s and was confirmed during the Easter Vigil in St. Philip's Cathedral, Atlanta, in the spring of 1986. As a new Episcopalian I visited numerous Episcopal churches, wishing to experience as many different Episcopal congregations as possible as I got to know my new church. Over thirty years ago, in Christ Church, Charlotte, North Carolina, I attended my first

Trinity Sunday service. The preacher was Frank Vest, Bishop of Southern Virginia and a former rector of the parish. Christ Church, Charlotte, is beautiful in its intentionally austere interior design. Several years after my initial visit, a friend of mine who was serving on the staff of Christ Church began my guided tour with: "Welcome to New England!"

All these years later I can still remember the lead-in to the sermon on that Trinity Sunday. Bishop Vest asked everyone to pick a window (the windows in Christ Church are clear glass) and to look through it. Look *through* the window, he said. And what do we see? We see a bit of creation. We get a glimpse of what the world is like. He went on to make the point that a window gives us a *glimpse*, a hint, a sense of what is outside. He then went on to say: Think of the doctrine of the Trinity as a window. Do not be daunted by its theological complexities. The doctrine of the Trinity is a *window* through which we get a glimpse, a hint, a taste—a sense—of the glory of God. Thirty plus years is a long time to remember the lead-in to a sermon. That sermon made a significant, indeed, a lasting impact on me. What a simple yet insightful and instructive suggestion: *Think of the doctrine of the Trinity as a window...*

Mark Oakley says in a Trinity Sunday sermon: "Today is the day put aside in the year to look at the portrait of God we call the Trinity."[1] In addition to looking *through* a *window*, we can look *at* the *portrait* of God offered in the doctrine of the Trinity. Trinity Sunday is the day in the Christian year when we stop to consider Trinitarian doctrine as a *window* into God, a *portrait* of the God whom we gather to worship and then go back into the world to serve.

The book I am currently reading is *1776* by David McCullough, one of our great public historians. Summer 2020 is an interesting point in our history to be reading a book about 1776 and the ideals of a brand-new nation coming to birth—our experiment in democracy. The book is mostly text, but there are also pictures of some of the leading figures of the Revolutionary era, such as George Washington, Nathanael Greene, John Adams, Thomas Jefferson, and King George III. The portraits add significantly to the text. After all, we do not have film of these people. We do not have photos of them. From a visual standpoint, all that we have are portraits. The portraits serve as *windows* into who these people were and offer us a *glimpse* of that formative time in our national history. The portraits tell us something important about the people and the period, they offer us a *sense* of the people and of the times in which they lived. No portrait can say everything, and yet they are invaluable resources.

It was sometime around Trinity Sunday during my first year of ordained ministry when a senior member of the parish—senior in every way, in age, tenure and authority(!)—called and said: "I have a problem I need to see you about." We then made an appointment for several days hence. Given my youth and inexperience, given his seniority in the parish, and given my predisposition to anxiety, in the days leading up to the appointment I wondered anxiously: What have I done wrong? What kind of trouble am I in? What's the problem? When the day of the appointment finally arrived and we settled in for our conversation, the man said: "Joel, my problem is this: I'm afraid I don't fully understand the doctrine of the Trinity." *That's the problem*? I then took a deep breath, exhaled a sigh of relief, and offered a response which I can remember to this day: "Well, I'd be more concerned about you if you thought you *did* fully understand the doctrine of the Trinity."

Martyn Percy writes in a Trinity Sunday sermon: "...the true Christian response to the mystery of the Trinity is not theology or philosophy, but worship. The complexity of the doctrinal formulae points beyond itself. God cannot be seen; His nature is hidden; truth is only dimly perceived."[2] Percy's point is that the doctrine of the Trinity exists to point *beyond itself* to the Mystery of God. The doctrine is a *window*, a *portrait*, essential to us but, in the end, a signpost pointing beyond itself to Mystery. Percy goes on: "...it is in worshipping the Trinity, not understanding it, that you begin to enter the divine matrix."[3]

Christians gather on Trinity Sunday, as on every other Sunday, to worship the Mystery behind our image(s) of God, our portrait(s) of God as Father, Son, and Holy Spirit—Creator, Redeemer, Sustainer. In our passage there is that profoundly interesting reference in Matthew 28:17: "When they saw him, they worshiped him; but some doubted." Most commentators on Matthew spend a significant amount of time on this one verse: "...they worshiped him; but some doubted." The Greek word rendered as "doubted" can also be translated as "hesitated." Scholars are clear that in context neither "doubted" nor "hesitated" in any way connotes a complete lack of faith. It is not that the disciples did not believe that Jesus was risen, but that they were overwhelmed by the *Mystery* of it all. Imagine having been there in real time, without the benefit of hindsight, without 2,000 years' worth of history and theology at our disposal. Imagine experiencing the resurrection firsthand. *When they saw him, they worshiped him; but some doubted.* It has been suggested that the disciples were experiencing cognitive dissonance *par excellence* and were simply unable to process what they were seeing. In 24:41, Luke, in his account of Easter evening, makes a similar point to Matthew's: "While in their joy they were disbelieving and still wondering..." The disciples experiencing the resurrection in real time were no doubt thrilled at one level and yet were aware that they were in the midst of something beyond their understanding—*Mystery* too deep for words.

A toweringly important passage in the Old Testament is Isaiah 55:8-9: "For my thoughts are not your thoughts, nor are your ways my ways, says the LORD. For as the heavens are higher than the earth, so are my ways higher than your ways and my thoughts than your thoughts." In 1 Corinthians 13:12 Paul puts it: "For now we see in a mirror, dimly, but then we will see face to face. Now I know only in part; then I will know fully, even as I have been fully known." Isaiah in the Hebrew Scriptures and Paul in the New Testament both remind us of our fundamental orientation of humility in response to Mystery.

When we are honest about it, we recognize that our understanding of truth is always only partial, and that we are meant to spend our lives growing in understanding. Throughout our lives we are, sometimes subtly and sometimes dramatically, experiencing changes in how we see and how we think. We are meant always to be evolving. We learn as we go. And most of us come to understand that the more we learn, the less we 'know,' and that increased 'knowledge' leads to a deeper humility. The more we learn, the more we experience and recognize the complexities of life and come to realize that, far more often than not, issues can be seen much more in terms of shades of gray rather than being simply black or white.

When we went into social distancing mode and started worshiping online back in the middle of March, we said then, and we say now, that we will be guided by the best medical advice. Of course, the best medical advice changes, it evolves over time. Our best medical experts know that this is a new, a novel coronavirus, and they know that they do not know what they do not know. And for all of the frustration of sometimes mixed messaging, at the same time it has been refreshing to see these brilliant scientists show humility in the face of this new and evolving challenge.

In the last week and a half, I have had to wrestle with my own understanding of issues of race in this country in the aftermath of the death of George Floyd and the resulting tsunami of social protests. Though my stance on race in my late 50s is nearly unrecognizable to what it would have been in my youth, or even in my young adulthood, during the last week and a half I have had to rethink again my fundamental understandings on issues of race. Even in the last week and a half my views have further evolved, changed. Life teaches us to have an increasingly open mind. We are always meant to be growing in our understanding of what it means to be human, and growing in our desire to reflect to one another the love of God made known to us most fully in Christ.

Trinity Sunday is the only Major Feast in the church's calendar that honors a doctrine, not a person or an event. The only one. It took the church between 300 and 400 years to come to 'agreement' on the doctrine of the Trinity—longer than the United States of America has existed as a nation. The doctrine of the Trinity is a window, a portrait—an invitation to respond to our Source, whom we regard as loving, compassionate, concerned and involved with and, ultimately, guiding our daily existence. Trinitarian language exists to point *beyond itself* to Mystery. Mark Oakley's mentor, Michael Mayne (1929-2006), 'frames' the portrait thusly: We were made by Love for love.

Every invitation we receive invites a response. Put more strongly, every invitation demands a response. And we do respond, in one way or another. We can accept. We can decline. We can ignore. But in the end we must respond. The doctrine of the Trinity is an invitation to a response to Love. Again, Mark Oakley: "Today is the day put aside in the year to look at the portrait of God we call the Trinity." And what might our response be to the invitation of Trinity Sunday? Oakley suggests: "Your life is a gift. Your life is an act of reckless generosity to which you are asked to respond with everything you have."[4] Amen.

CHAPTER THIRTEEN

GUT-LEVEL COMPASSION

14 June 2020 • Matthew 9:35–10:8

[35] Jesus went about all the cities and villages, teaching in their synagogues, and proclaiming the good news of the kingdom, and curing every disease and every sickness. [36] When he saw the crowds, he had compassion for them, because they were harassed and helpless, like sheep without a shepherd. [37] Then he said to his disciples, "The harvest is plentiful, but the laborers are few; [38] therefore ask the Lord of the harvest to send out laborers into his harvest."

[1] Then Jesus summoned his twelve disciples and gave them authority over unclean spirits, to cast them out, and to cure every disease and every sickness. [2] These are the names of the twelve apostles: first, Simon, also known as Peter, and his brother Andrew; James son of Zebedee, and his brother John; [3] Philip and Bartholomew; Thomas and Matthew the tax collector; James son of Alphaeus, and Thaddaeus; [4] Simon the Cananaean, and Judas Iscariot, the one who betrayed him. [5] These twelve Jesus sent out with the following instructions: "Go nowhere among the Gentiles, and enter no town of the

Samaritans, ⁶ but go rather to the lost sheep of the house of Israel. ⁷ As you go, proclaim the good news, 'The kingdom of heaven has come near.' ⁸ Cure the sick, raise the dead, cleanse the lepers, cast out demons. You received without payment; give without payment."

Matthew 9:36: "When he saw the crowds, he had compassion for them, because they were harassed and helpless, like sheep without a shepherd." Here we encounter one of the most memorable and moving verses in all of the Gospels. "Compassion" is a proper translation of the Greek. It is also a polite translation. The literal meaning of the Greek is "viscera." The word refers to our internal organs, our innards. When Jesus saw the crowds, he had *compassion* for them... He was moved to the very core of his being.

Commenting on verse 36, Craig L. Blomberg notes: "Jesus' human emotions reflect a deep, *gut-level* 'compassion'..."¹ *The New English Bible* translates: "The sight of the people moved him to pity..." For "harassed and helpless" the New American Standard Bible has: "distressed and dispirited." Here again, these are proper translations, but they are also polite in tone. The Greek here for "harassed and helpless" is literally: "mangled and torn asunder," which makes the last clause of verse 36 make perfect sense. It can be read: *When he saw the crowds, he had compassion for them, for they were mangled and torn asunder, like sheep without a shepherd.* Surely this is indeed one of the most memorable and moving verses in all the Gospels. Matthew exercises his every literary muscle to convey Jesus' offer of a deep, gut-level compassion for those in need.

During this time of social distancing, we are offering Morning Prayer as our liturgy on Sundays. Of course, in more normal times we would be celebrating the Holy Eucharist. When celebrating the Holy Eucharist, early on in the liturgy we pray the Collect for Purity: "Almighty God, to you all hearts are open, all desires known, and from you no secrets are hid: Cleanse the thoughts of our hearts by the inspiration of your Holy Spirit, that we may perfectly love you, and worthily magnify your holy Name..."[2] Beautiful words, and to many of us they are quite familiar. In fact, for many of us they may be so familiar that we can hear the words during a celebration of Holy Eucharist without really *hearing* them.

Angus Ritchie writes regarding the Collect for Purity: "In [it]...we ask God to cleanse the thoughts of our hearts, and not of our heads. This cleansing is not about having an inner life that is free from all upheaval and disturbance. The unclean state of our hearts is often revealed by complacency and emotional disconnection from suffering. It is because Christ has a clean heart that he is moved to the very depths of his being by the plight of God's people."[3] The unclean state of our hearts is in fact often revealed by *complacency* and *emotional disconnection* from suffering.

Since the beginning of the pandemic, I have noticed something in the media both at the local level and at the national level, and with regard both to television and radio. Numerous times during these last few weeks I have heard: "We're *all* hunkered down in our houses." Or: "We're *all* bored being cooped up in our houses." Or: "We *all* have cabin fever." Well, in reality we are not *all* hunkered down in our houses. And in reality, we are not *all* bored. Not *all of us* have cabin fever! From the beginning of our battle with COVID-19, there have been countless people working tirelessly on the front lines—doctors, nurses, medical technicians, cleaning staff, police, firefighters, EMTs and other first responders, people who work in grocery stores and in food preparation in restaurants and cafeterias. The list could go on and on. We are not *all* tired of being hunkered down! Not all of us have a place to hunker. And we are not *all* bored. For so many people, every day is a struggle to survive. We do not *all* have cabin fever. This kind of too-casual rhetoric displays a disconnection from people's suffering. We are always meant to be careful about our language.

Again, Angus Ritchie, reflecting on the Collect for Purity in the context of Matthew 9:35-10:8:

> In the Collect for Purity we ask God to cleanse the thoughts of our hearts, and not of our heads. This cleansing is not about having an inner life that is free from all upheaval and disturbance. The unclean state of our hearts is often revealed by complacency and emotional disconnection from suffering. It is because Christ has a clean heart that he is moved to the very depths of his being by the plight of God's people.

Underneath the ongoing protests following the deaths of Ahmaud Arbery and George Floyd is a crying out against complacency, a crying out against emotional disconnection from suffering. And in the moment that is now, this crying out must be heard by *all*. The compassion to which Jesus calls us is characterized by both gut-level emotion *and* appropriate, 'connected' action.

After services on Trinity Sunday last week, John Sentamu retired as Archbishop of York. John Sentamu has served as Archbishop of York since 2005. He was born in Uganda, and was briefly imprisoned by the Amin regime, escaping in 1974. Before he fled the country as a political refugee, John Sentamu was a judge in the court system in Uganda. In time, he became Bishop of Stepney (1996-2002) in the Diocese of London. Sentamu then became Bishop of Birmingham (2002-05), and subsequently was consecrated Archbishop of York (2005).

Throughout his ministry, John Sentamu has been an evangelist, and he has campaigned tirelessly for social justice. In a tribute to John Sentamu in *Church Times*, John Barton, a former advisor to Archbishop Sentamu, tells the story that when Sentamu was Bishop of Birmingham, he made a pastoral visit to the city's central mosque. Barton tells the story that in greeting the people in the central mosque in Birmingham, one of the most diverse cities in Europe, John Sentamu said: "I greet you in the name of Jesus Christ—to you, a prophet, but, for me, my Lord and Saviour."[4]

Soon after his installation as Archbishop of York, John Sentamu was hosting a public gathering. After his talk there was a time for questions and answers, and in the Q and A there came a moment when a little boy spoke up and asked the newly consecrated Archbishop of York: "Why do you believe in God?" Out of the mouths of babes! To the newly consecrated *Archbishop of York*, from a little boy in the crowd: *Why do you believe in God?* Barton tells us that Archbishop Sentamu beckoned the little boy to come up, and, as the child approached, Sentamu realized that one of the boy's shoelaces was untied. So the newly consecrated Archbishop of York knelt down and tied this little boy's shoelaces. And then he said in response to the child's question: "When I was a boy someone told me that Jesus could be my friend. So, that night I knelt by my bed and asked Jesus to be my friend. And do you know something? He is still my friend."[5]

When he saw the crowds, he had compassion for them, because they were harassed and helpless, like sheep without a shepherd. Amen.

CHAPTER FOURTEEN

OUR REMEDY IS THE GRACE OF CHRIST

5 July 2020 • Matthew 11:16-19, 25-30

[16] Jesus said, "But to what will I compare this generation? It is like children sitting in the marketplaces and calling to one another, [17] 'We played the flute for you, and you did not dance; we wailed, and you did not mourn.' [18] For John came neither eating nor drinking, and they say, 'He has a demon'; [19] the Son of Man came eating and drinking, and they say, 'Look, a glutton and a drunkard, a friend of tax collectors and sinners!' Yet wisdom is vindicated by her deeds." [25] At that time Jesus said, "I thank you, Father, Lord of heaven and earth, because you have hidden these things from the wise and the intelligent and have revealed them to infants; [26] yes, Father, for such was your gracious will. [27] All things have been handed over to me by my Father; and no one knows the Son except the Father, and no one knows the Father except the Son and anyone to whom the Son chooses to reveal him. [28] "Come to me, all you that are weary and are carrying heavy burdens, and I will give you rest. [29] Take my yoke upon you, and learn from me; for I am gentle and

humble in heart, and you will find rest for your souls. [30] For my yoke is easy, and my burden is light."

I have a memory from my teenage years of regularly reading in my hometown newspaper the daily column by Dr. Billy Graham. I have a specific memory of a particular correspondent writing to Dr. Graham: *Reverend Graham, I think I may have violated one of the Ten Commandments. What should I do?* All these years later I can remember Billy Graham's response: *Friend, if you take a closer look at your life, I suspect you will find that you may have broken more than one of the Ten Commandments.*

The Judeo-Christian tradition's moral and ethical underpinnings are the Ten Commandments. *Ten.* But by Jesus' lifetime, in the hundreds of years since the Ten Commandments were originally received, rabbinic teaching had expanded the original Ten Commandments to 613. We think of the *Ten* Commandments and know that we cannot possibly achieve moral or ethical perfection. We regularly violate more than one of the Ten Commandments. Just imagine trying to keep 613. Of course, the expansion of the Ten Commandments was done with good intentions—to further clarify right from wrong—but over hundreds of years additions to the law kept accumulating under the assumption: the more guidance, the better.

Jesus' original hearers would have known the term: the "yoke" of the law. The phrase comes into play in Matthew 11:16-19, 25-30. The rabbis referred to the *yoke* of the law which they meant in a positive sense: *the more guidance, the better.* But for the populace in general, many people had come to find the 'weight' of the law burdensome and frustrating, too layered and complex. Jesus, in his wisdom, understood the people's frustration, and, in his wisdom, knew that in many cases, less is more, and that spiritual principles are meant to be life-giving, not burdensome and sources of frustration.

I will never forget receiving an email from a friend, a retired progressive Baptist pastor who lives in Australia. The email contained the words of a truism he had encountered on a poster in the halls of a hospital in Adelaide: "Joy is the infallible sign of the presence of God." I printed a copy of that line and have it taped to the inside of my office door so that I can be reminded every day: *Joy is the infallible sign of the presence of God.* In this context, joy is not the same as happiness. *Happiness* tends to come and go, moment to moment, depending on one's circumstances. *Joy* speaks of a deeper, more foundational sense of connection with God. I once encountered a definition of joy which I carry with me to this day: *Joy is being where we are meant to be, doing what we are meant to do.*

Though joy and happiness are clearly related, in the end they are not synonyms. Joy refers to our deep, abiding sense of connection to our Source, and Jesus came to convey the message that God's will for us is to be in joyful, peaceful, life-giving relationship with the Divine, and not to find the spiritual life so layered and complex that the law itself—its moral and ethical guidelines—becomes a source of frustration and anxiety. Jesus says in Matthew 11:25: "I thank you, Father, Lord of heaven and earth, because you have hidden these things from the wise and the intelligent and have revealed them to infants..." This is Jesus' way of calling us back to a childlike faith, a faith based on simple, though not simplistic, trust: trust that we are beloved children of a God of love—that we were made by Love, for love.

In verse 28 we read: "Come to me, all you that are weary and are carrying heavy burdens..." This is a reference to the people's frustration with the legalism of the day. "Come to me, all you that are weary and are carrying heavy burdens, and I will give you rest. Take my yoke upon you..." As was noted earlier, people knew the phrase, the "yoke" of the law. Jesus takes that phrase and gives it a new, more positive twist. "Take *my yoke* (emphasis mine) upon you, and learn from me; for I am *gentle and humble* (emphasis mine) in heart, and you will find *rest* (emphasis mine) for your souls. For *my yoke* (emphasis mine) is easy, and *my burden is light* (emphasis mine)." "Yoke" here is redefined. Jesus' message was and is: Relationship with God is not about constantly striving to reach moral or ethical perfection. Spirituality is not about putting so much pressure on ourselves to be 'perfect' that the joy of spirituality dissipates. Jesus' message was revolutionary in spiritual terms: Come to *me*, and I will show you a more generous path to spiritual peace and fulfillment. N.T. Wright says in a summary statement about our passage that it is: "...still the most welcoming and encouraging invitation ever offered."[1]

It is important to note that, in the end, Jesus' message is not an invitation to inactivity or passivity. We *are* to work in our daily lives to make the love of God known. We have much to do in order to proclaim God's love in both word and deed. Jesus' gracious invitation is not a call to retreat from the hard realities of daily life. It is, however, an invitation to face these realities in terms of God's love—with humility, and yet with a strong sense of purpose. Jesus invites us into a spirituality of healthy humility. His desire for us is not moral or ethical perfection, but humble, faithful commitment to sharing God's love in the world. Our actions in the name of Christ are to be undertaken not in order to prove our own worthiness, but with a servant's heart. Again, Matthew 11:29a: "Take my yoke upon you..." Jesus' original hearers would have understood what he meant. They would have known the phrase: *the yoke of the law*. Jesus' invitation is a gracious, loving invitation into a relationship of trust with himself and the Father. Robert H. Mounce writes in his summary comment on our passage: "It is to these who would approach God in the simplicity of personal trust that Jesus promises rest."[2]

One of the towering figures of early Christian history is Ambrose of Milan (ca. 339 - 97 AD). Ambrose is one of the great theologians in the history of the Christian Church. He is also remembered as having been a mentor to St. Augustine of Hippo (354–430 AD), arguably Christianity's greatest theologian. Ambrose of Milan, from the fourth century, offers: "We have a physician. Let us follow his remedy. Our remedy is the grace of Christ." Amen.

CHAPTER FIFTEEN

DIFFERENT FACETS OF GOD'S GLORY

Matthew 13:24-30, 36-43 • 19 July 2020

[24] He put before them another parable: "The kingdom of heaven may be compared to someone who sowed good seed in his field; [25] but while everybody was asleep, an enemy came and sowed weeds among the wheat, and then went away. [26] So when the plants came up and bore grain, then the weeds appeared as well. [27] And the slaves of the householder came and said to him, 'Master, did you not sow good seed in your field? Where, then, did these weeds come from?' [28] He answered, 'An enemy has done this.' The slaves said to him, 'Then do you want us to go and gather them?' [29] But he replied, 'No; for in gathering the weeds you would uproot the wheat along with them. [30] Let both of them grow together until the harvest; and at harvest time I will tell the reapers, Collect the weeds first and bind them in bundles to be burned, but gather the wheat into my barn.'"

[36] Then he left the crowds and went into the house. And his disciples approached him, saying, "Explain to us the parable of the weeds of the field." [37] He answered, "The one who sows the good seed is the Son of Man; [38] the field is the world, and the

good seed are the children of the kingdom; the weeds are the children of the evil one, [39] and the enemy who sowed them is the devil; the harvest is the end of the age, and the reapers are angels. [40] Just as the weeds are collected and burned up with fire, so will it be at the end of the age. [41] The Son of Man will send his angels, and they will collect out of his kingdom all causes of sin and all evildoers, [42] and they will throw them into the furnace of fire, where there will be weeping and gnashing of teeth. [43] Then the righteous will shine like the sun in the kingdom of their Father. Let anyone with ears listen!"

In his commentary on the Parable of the Wheat and the Tares, William Barclay tells the true story of two men in civilian clothes having lunch together in a cafe in London during World War I. One of the two men was Collie Knox, who would rise to fame in World War II as a war correspondent; during World War I he was a young airman in the RAF. While Collie Knox and a friend were having lunch in civilian clothes a young woman came up to them and offered each of them a white feather, a symbol of cowardice. Her assumption was that these two young men were not serving their country during wartime. What she did not know was that Collie Knox was recovering from an injury suffered in a crash during his service in the RAF, and his lunch companion had just come from Buckingham Palace where he had been awarded a commendation for bravery in combat. In telling the story Barclay notes: "It is the easiest thing in the world to judge completely wrongly."[1] Surely we all can think of times (plural!) when we have been mistaken and have judged prematurely, when we have spoken or acted before we had all the facts. It *is* the easiest thing in the world to judge completely wrongly.

The Parable of the Wheat and the Tares is one of Jesus' most memorable parables. The essentials of the parable are clear. There is a landowner who sows good seed. An enemy comes in and sows weeds among the good seed in an act we might call industrial sabotage. Servants become concerned and offer to pull the weeds from amidst the good crop. The problem with that is that the weeds and the good crop look identical in their early stages of development, and over time the roots of the weeds become intertwined, interconnected, with the roots of the good seed. In verse 30a the landowner says: "Let both of them grow together until the harvest..." In the end, what we have here is a parable teaching us about the necessity and the importance of waiting, and patience.

At various times, and in various ways, Jesus teaches us about waiting, about the value of patience. Throughout his ministry Jesus warned against judgmentalism. He repeatedly cautions his hearers against condemning people prematurely and standing in judgment of others without having all the facts. It is a recurring theme with Jesus: "Let anyone among you who is without sin be the first to throw a stone..."[2]

Paul echoes this recurrent theme. He writes in 1 Corinthians 4:5: "Therefore do not pronounce judgment before the time, before the Lord comes, who will bring to light the things now hidden in darkness and will disclose the purposes of the heart." Paul also cautions in Romans 12:16b: "...do not claim to be wiser than you are."

The Parable of the Wheat and the Tares teaches us about the importance of waiting when circumstances require it. It teaches us about *patience*. The parable warns against the all too prevalent human tendency to judge, to label and to create divisions—to categorize prematurely without enough factual information. Such teaching about patience and waiting, about non-judgmentalism, leads us to consider the importance of humility. Again Paul's teaching: Do not claim to be wiser than you are.

In his commentary on the parable, William Barclay talks about Jesus offering "wide welcome."[3] Jesus went from village to village, town to town, person to person, offering a wide welcome, for which he was frequently criticized. Repeatedly in the Gospels, we see Pharisees being critical of Jesus' openness to those whom some would have written off as 'sinners,' as 'unrighteous.' In the Gospels, Pharisees tend repeatedly to be critical of Jesus' offer of inclusion. That said, at times his own disciples are confused by Jesus' offer of wide welcome. At times, even his disciples instinctively question: Are we really reaching out to *these* people?

Earlier in Matthew 13 we have the Parable of the Sower. The sower sows in all types of soil and is generous in spreading the seed. Then in 13:47 we read: "...the kingdom of heaven is like a net that was thrown into the sea and caught fish of every kind..." The teaching of the Parable of the Wheat and the Tares and the Parable of the Sower is, in the end, clear. As followers of Jesus we are to spread the seed, we are to sow the 'seed' of the Gospel. We are to share the Good News far and wide. We are to 'cast the net' and keep casting it in graciousness—invitingly—not pre-determining in our minds who is likely to receive the invitation, or who is worthy. Ours is to sow the seed, to cast the net widely. Following the example of Jesus, ours is to offer a wide welcome.

John Adams and Thomas Jefferson are two of the Founders of our nation. Though long-time friends, owing to substantive policy disagreements theirs was not always an easy relationship. Adams of Massachusetts, and Jefferson of Virginia held quite different views in some important areas. Yet they worked together for years and were, in the end, friends. In his maturity, Adams wrote to Jefferson and observed: "My friend, you and I have lived in serious times."[4]

In a technology-driven, interconnected world that neither Adams nor Jefferson could have imagined, in 2020 we find ourselves in serious times. Some of us who made it to the ball drop on New Year's Eve heard in real time the familiar New Year's greeting: "Happy New Year!" In those first moments of the New Year, we could not have imagined what our lives would look like in July. Owing to the pandemic, there is a growing fatigue in our culture, a spreading fear. And we are living in a time of heightened social tensions that force us to recognize that the American Dream is and always has been aspirational, a work in progress.

Many of us who grew up in church were taught at a young age a very basic definition of parables: A parable is an earthly story with a heavenly meaning. In the end, the Parable of the Wheat and the Tares is not really about agriculture. Jesus uses accessible, familiar language to teach us about patience, about perseverance. And, in the same parable, he teaches us about non-judgmentalism. The parable teaches us to be slow in reaching judgment about an individual, or a group of people whom we do not know and whose story is not our own.

In his commentary on the parable, N.T. Wright observes: "Since we're all different, God intends that each of us should reflect a different facet of his glory."[5] The Parable of the Wheat and the Tares is deceptively simple. In the end, its 'simple' language is as instructive and as relevant today as it ever has been. As effectively as any other of Jesus' teachings, the parable cautions us to be slow to judge, slow to place people in categories, slow to label people before we even know them.

Like John Adams and Thomas Jefferson in their day, we are living in serious times. The challenge, *and* the opportunity before us in this season of social stirring is to come to see our differences not as the source of intractable and endless conflict. Rather, step by step, day by day, conversation after conversation, this serious time invites us—challenges us—to see our diversity as different facets of God's glory and the makings of a beautiful mosaic. Amen.

CHAPTER SIXTEEN

THE LIVING TABLETS OF OUR HEARTS

Romans 8:26-39 • 26 July 2020

26 The Spirit helps us in our weakness; for we do not know how to pray as we ought, but that very Spirit intercedes with sighs too deep for words. 27 And God, who searches the heart, knows what is the mind of the Spirit, because the Spirit intercedes for the saints according to the will of God. 28 We know that all things work together for good for those who love God, who are called according to his purpose. 29 For those whom he foreknew he also predestined to be conformed to the image of his Son, in order that he might be the firstborn within a large family. 30 And those whom he predestined he also called; and those whom he called he also justified; and those whom he justified he also glorified. 31 What then are we to say about these things? If God is for us, who is against us? 32 He who did not withhold his own Son, but gave him up for all of us, will he not with him also give us everything else? 33 Who will bring any charge against God's elect? It is God who justifies. 34 Who is to condemn? It is Christ Jesus, who died, yes, who was raised,

who is at the right hand of God, who indeed intercedes for us.
[35] Who will separate us from the love of Christ? Will hardship,
or distress, or persecution, or famine, or nakedness, or peril, or
sword? [36] As it is written, "For your sake we are being killed all
day long; we are accounted as sheep to be slaughtered." [37] No,
in all these things we are more than conquerors through him
who loved us. [38] For I am convinced that neither death, nor life,
nor angels, nor rulers, nor things present, nor things to come,
nor powers, [39] nor height, nor depth, nor anything else in all
creation, will be able to separate us from the love of God in
Christ Jesus our Lord.

Between the time of his conversion experience and the
time in which he wrote the Epistle to the Romans, ca.
58 AD, Paul had spent years in missionary and pastoral
work, and thus what we have in the Epistle to the Romans is the
fruit of a mature mind. In his commentary on Romans, C. H.
Dodd (1884-1973), one of the great Bible scholars of the twentieth century, notes that Paul evinced a first-rate mind and was a
man of "the deepest spiritual insight."[1] Another leading scholar,
Leander Keck, writes: "What gives Romans its depth and
power...is the rigor of Paul's own thought."[2] And C.K. Barrett
observes regarding Romans 8:26-39 that it is "...full of
passionate eloquence..."[3] Barrett doubtless has chosen the word
"passionate" here with intention and care. Paul's thinking in
Romans comes from a deep place. Every word intended for the
church in Rome has been carefully considered and chosen.

In her wonderfully titled book, *When in Romans: An Invitation
to Linger with the Gospel according to Paul*, Beverly Roberts Gaventa
writes of our passage that it is filled with "soaring language."[4]
And N.T. Wright says of the passage that it offers "a thrilling
rhetorical statement."[5] In 8:31-32 Paul writes: "What then are
we to say about these things? If God is for us, who is against us?
He who did not withhold his own Son, but gave him up for all of

us, will he not with him also give us everything else?" Here we are reminded of Paul's claim in 5:8: "But God proves his love for us in that while we still were sinners Christ died for us."

In 8:35 we encounter some of the most memorable wording in all of the New Testament: "Who will separate us from the love of Christ? Will hardship, or distress, or persecution, or famine, or nakedness, or peril, or sword?" Paul could claim to have experienced most or all of these conditions: hardship, distress, persecution, famine, nakedness, peril, and the threat of the sword. In reflecting on Romans in *Africa Bible Commentary*, David M. Kasali writes of Paul's rhetoric in 8:35: "Having looked at everything in life..."[6] Having looked at *everything*... By the time he wrote the Epistle to the Romans, Paul had pretty much seen it all and lived it all. What we have on offer in Romans is the distillation of years of maturity and pastoral experience. The Epistle to the Romans is written with a voice of authority.

The church in Rome in the late 50s AD was a tiny minority sect in a vast cosmopolitan city hostile to the Judeo-Christian tradition. The Roman historian Suetonius (ca. 69 - ca. 122 AD) tells us that in 49 AD, Christians and Jews were expelled from Rome by the Emperor Claudius and that only after Claudius was murdered (54 AD) could Jews and Christians return to the city. Thus, Paul is writing to a church that understands what it is like to live in a hostile culture. Paul himself knew perfectly well the dangers and the challenges that faced the church in Rome. It is into this dramatic historical context that Paul writes in 8:31b: "If God is for us, who is against us?" And in 8:35a: "Who will separate us from the love of Christ?" And then in 8:37: "...in all these things we are more than conquerors through him who loved us." To the church in first-century Rome, hardly the most favorable environment for the flourishing of the Judeo-Christian tradition, Paul writes with *passionate eloquence*, employing *soaring language*. Paul's message to the Christians in Rome is that, regardless of our circumstances, we are never beyond the reach of God's love.

Scholars agree that our passage serves as a summary of the contents of the epistle up to this point. In the ensuing verse, 9:1, Paul shifts gears. C.K. Barrett, one of the great Pauline scholars of any era, writes that the message of chapters 1-8 is: "...the grounds of Christian hope."[7] Barrett goes on to note that chapters 1-8 serve as a road map for "...Christian *action* (emphasis mine) in the present."[8]

Just one brief reminder about Paul's biography. We first meet him as Saul, a Pharisee, and a persecutor of Christians. We are told in Acts 7:58 that Saul was present at the stoning of Stephen, the first Christian martyr, and that Stephen's persecutors laid their cloaks at the feet of Saul. Luke clearly tells us that Saul was complicit in the stoning of Stephen, but, though once a persecutor of Christians, through his life-changing conversion— his experience of the risen Christ—Paul's entire life is turned around, and he becomes the great champion of the Good News of Jesus Christ risen and active in the world.

Following his conversion, and after years of missionary and pastoral work, in writing the Epistle to the Romans Paul really has seen it all. He has lived it all. It is from this foundation that Paul writes with such passionate eloquence, and in such soaring language: "For I am convinced that neither death, nor life, nor angels, nor rulers, nor things present, nor things to come, nor powers, nor height, nor depth, nor anything else in all creation, will be able to separate us from the love of God in Christ Jesus our Lord." To the church in Rome, still carving out its existence in the midst of a hostile culture, Paul, in his personal and spiritual maturity, assures this minority congregation that God's love can be trusted and felt even in the most trying of circumstances: reassuring and sustaining good news for the Christians in Rome in the late 50s AD, and for us facing our own challenges in 2020. A part of what it means to be a Christian is to have the assurance: *Nothing* can separate us from the love of God in Christ.

Using his own soaring language, and writing with his own passionate eloquence, N.T. Wright comments on today's epistle lesson: "The end of Romans 8 deserves to be written in letters of fire on the living tablets of our hearts."[9] Amen.

CHAPTER SEVENTEEN

FOR THERE IS NO DISTINCTION

9 August 2020 • Romans 10:5-15

⁵ Moses writes concerning the righteousness that comes from the law, that "the person who does these things will live by them." ⁶ But the righteousness that comes from faith says, "Do not say in your heart, 'Who will ascend into heaven?'" (that is, to bring Christ down) ⁷ "or 'Who will descend into the abyss?'" (that is, to bring Christ up from the dead). ⁸ But what does it say? "The word is near you, on your lips and in your heart" (that is, the word of faith that we proclaim); ⁹ because if you confess with your lips that Jesus is Lord and believe in your heart that God raised him from the dead, you will be saved. ¹⁰ For one believes with the heart and so is justified, and one confesses with the mouth and so is saved. ¹¹ The scripture says, "No one who believes in him will be put to shame." ¹² For there is no distinction between Jew and Greek; the same Lord is Lord of all and is generous to all who call on him. ¹³ For, "Everyone who calls on the name of the Lord shall be saved." ¹⁴ But how are they to call on one in whom they have not believed? And how are they to believe in one of whom they have never heard?

And how are they to hear without someone to proclaim him? [15] And how are they to proclaim him unless they are sent? As it is written, "How beautiful are the feet of those who bring good news!"

"For there is no distinction between Jew and Greek; the same Lord is Lord of all and is generous to all who call on him." Paul makes this teaching even more specific in his Letter to the Galatians (3:27-28): "As many of you as were baptized into Christ have clothed yourselves with Christ. There is no longer Jew or Greek, there is no longer slave or free, there is no longer male and female; for all of you are one in Christ Jesus." Romans 10:12 builds on its preceding verse: "The scripture says, 'No one who believes in him will be put to shame'"— a reference to Isaiah 28:16. The teaching of 10:12 is then amplified in verse 13: "For, 'Everyone who calls on the name of the Lord shall be saved'"—a quotation from the prophet Joel (2:32).

Chapters 9-11 form a discrete section within the Epistle to the Romans dealing with the relationship of Jews and Gentiles. The Christian movement arose out of a Jewish context, and yet, by the time Paul wrote his letter to the Romans, Christianity's growth was spreading primarily in Gentile territory. Romans 9-11 deals with the question: What is the status of God's relationship with the Jews, given that Christianity is spreading more rapidly among Gentiles? And, relatedly, given the fact that Christianity arose out of a Jewish context, are Gentiles somehow 'second class citizens' as latecomers? These were profound questions in the first century. The world was not a global village. Barriers between races, ethnicities and languages were more pronounced then than now. It was a foundational question for Paul to address: Can the church include both Jews and Gentiles as coequals? Paul answers the question in Romans 10:11-13: "The scripture says, 'No one who believes in him will be put to shame.' For there is no distinction between Jew and

Greek; the same Lord is Lord of all and is generous to all who call on him. For 'Everyone who calls on the name of the Lord shall be saved.'"

One of the great Bible scholars of the twentieth century was C.H. Dodd (1884-1973). In 1932, among three books that Dodd published that year was a commentary on Romans, a classic treatment that remains useful nearly 100 years after its publication. Reflecting on Paul's vision of unity, Dodd writes that Paul's vision is: "the logical implication of monotheism."[1] Paul's vision that people from different backgrounds *can* come together and live in unity and harmony is the *logical implication* of monotheism.

Romans 10 connects up with what Paul has said earlier in chapter 3. In Romans 3:22b-24 Paul writes: "For there is no distinction, since all have sinned and fall short of the glory of God; they are now justified by his grace as a gift, through the redemption that is in Christ Jesus." Matthew Black writes in his commentary on Romans that 3:22b-24 forms: "the central plank in the Pauline Gospel."[2] The *central plank* in the Pauline Gospel is his underlying idea of unity, the fundamental equality of all in the sight of God. Paul makes clear in Romans 3 that all have sinned. As sinners, we all live in 'glass houses.' That said, Paul also makes clear that all are equally able to receive grace, and that no group can stand in judgment over another group because all have sinned, and all may receive grace equally. Paul says it twice for emphasis, in 3:22 and 10:12: There is no distinction. We are all of equal value in the sight of God. This *is* the logical implication of monotheism.

For a man of his time, Paul was as cosmopolitan as was possible. He was of Jewish heritage, and yet he was a Roman citizen. Paul was a Pharisee, and had studied at the feet of Gamaliel, one of the great rabbis of the first century (Acts 22:3). In a first-century context, regarding diversity, the thorny, vexing challenges of people from disparate backgrounds coming together in unity and living in harmony—regarding racial, ethnic, socioeconomic, and theological diversity—Paul was uniquely placed to address these issues. And Paul uses his platform as an evangelist to speak with boldness and prophetic insight: *There is no distinction.* C.H. Dodd, writing in 1932, observed of Paul's vision of unity that it is the *logical implication of monotheism.* It was then, and it is now.

I heard a true story recently of a family with very little religious background going into a church building. We now have a category that sociologists of religion use for people with no religious affiliation: "Nones." Nones constitute a growing segment of our society. This family with no religious affiliation walked into a Christian church where over the altar hung a large, highly visible crucifix. A young child in the family, having no religious training, asked: "Why is that man hanging on a plus sign?"

The answer to the child's question is that Jesus hangs there for all of humanity. *Father, forgive them...* Jesus was nailed to a wooden cross on a specific date in history and in a particular place for the forgiveness of the sin of the world: his world, and for generations yet unborn. Jesus willingly went to the cross for his friends, his family, *and* his enemies.

In 2009, I had the privilege of a three-month sabbatical, and for one of those months was visiting preacher in St. Paul's Anglican Church, Athens, Greece. St. Paul's, Athens, is a parish of the Church of England (Diocese of Europe). The congregation is extraordinarily diverse. It appeared to me at the time that about sixty percent of the congregation were Africans from all over the continent. We also had people from Asia, South America, Europe, and just a handful of Americans, including a young woman from Calhoun, Georgia. After church one day this young woman came up to me during coffee hour and said: "I'm from Calhoun, Georgia, and I just loved hearin' you talk." To which I responded: "Well, I love hearin' you talk." The church wardens were two women: one, a wildly eccentric native of New Jersey, the other, a Nigerian named Magdalena. St. Paul's, Athens, is comprised of diplomats and their families, retirees, and refugees, both political and economic and, of course, British expatriates. And, as you can imagine, we would have visitors each week from all parts of the world who had sought out an Anglican church for worship.

I reemphasize that in the parish were a mere handful of Americans. On Sunday mornings I would look out over the congregation and think: What a beautiful sea of diversity this is, all worshiping *together*. It was an inspiring vision, a foretaste of Heaven. St. Paul's, Athens, must be just about as diverse a Christian congregation as exists anywhere in the world, and yet there is a wonderful sense of unity in that parish. Being there even for a month was a lifetime experience. For all of the obvious diversity present within the parish, we found *unity* in Christ. *For there is no distinction...*

"Why is that man hanging on a plus sign?" For us all. Amen.

CHAPTER EIGHTEEN
HOLDING HER GROUND

16 August 2020 • Matthew 15:21-28

[21] Jesus left that place and went away to the district of Tyre and Sidon. [22] Just then a Canaanite woman from that region came out and started shouting, "Have mercy on me, Lord, Son of David; my daughter is tormented by a demon." [23] But he did not answer her at all. And his disciples came and urged him, saying, "Send her away, for she keeps shouting after us." [24] He answered, "I was sent only to the lost sheep of the house of Israel." [25] But she came and knelt before him, saying, "Lord, help me." [26] He answered, "It is not fair to take the children's food and throw it to the dogs." [27] She said, "Yes, Lord, yet even the dogs eat the crumbs that fall from their masters' table." [28] Then Jesus answered her, "Woman, great is your faith! Let it be done for you as you wish." And her daughter was healed instantly.

W e all know what we mean by the words, "the smell test." We may say: It doesn't pass the smell test. Or: This just doesn't smell right. Of course, what is really being said is: Something just does not seem right. Something is missing. Something simply does not add up here.

We may think in terms of the smell test when we read Matthew 15:21-28. Matthew tells us that Jesus and his disciples have temporarily migrated to a Gentile region, Tyre and Sidon (modern-day Lebanon). Scholars estimate that they have undertaken a three days' journey on foot to get there. In 15:22 we meet a Canaanite woman—a Gentile. There are historical references to Canaanites going all the way back to 3,000 BC. Canaanites were the inhabitants of the area that the Jewish nation claimed as the Promised Land. Most Canaanites never converted to Judaism, leaving Canaanites and Jews as natural enemies.

In 15:22 the Canaanite woman approaches Jesus and says: "Have mercy on me, Lord, Son of David; my daughter is tormented by a demon." Notice how she addresses Jesus: *Lord, Son of David*. Somehow this woman has a sense of who Jesus is, a deeper sense in fact than some of his own people in his own nation. We are surprised when Matthew tells us: "But he did not answer her at all." This does not pass the smell test. It does not sound like Jesus. Then Matthew tells us: "And his disciples came and urged him, saying, 'Send her away, for she keeps shouting after us.'" Scholars debate exactly what is meant here. It could mean: *Give her what she wants* so that she will leave us alone. But more scholars think that what the disciples are saying here is: Teacher, *get rid of her*. She is annoying us.

To this Canaanite woman who has spoken to Jesus in terms of "Lord," and "Son of David," Matthew tells us: "He answered, 'I was sent only to the lost sheep of the house of Israel.'" At one level this makes sense. Jesus' ministry had a focus. He was Jewish. His cultural milieu was Judaism. To focus on the house of Israel would make all the sense in the world. We here at St. Luke's focus on Cleveland and Bradley County, but, of course, our concerns are not confined to our local setting. Already in chapter 8 of Matthew's narrative, Jesus has healed a Roman centurion's servant, and thus has already shown mercy to a Gentile. Looking ahead to the end of Matthew, in 28:19 we find the Great Commission: "Go therefore and make disciples of all nations, baptizing them in the name of the Father and of the Son and of the Holy Spirit."

Jesus' initial response to the Canaanite woman is: "I was sent only to the lost sheep of the house of Israel." Then Matthew continues: "But she came and knelt before him, saying, 'Lord, help me.'" The Greek here for "knelt" is the same word from which we get "worship," and thus *knelt* here can connote a sense of prayerfulness and reverence. This Canaanite mother makes an exceedingly understandable request: Lord, help me. My daughter is suffering.

Then Matthew tells us: "He answered, 'It is not fair to take the children's food and throw it to the dogs.'" In his commentary on our passage, Robert H. Mounce writes: "*Dog* was a common Jewish term for Gentiles based on their making no distinction between clean and unclean foods."[1] Most dogs will eat 'anything,' and thus the slur against Gentiles who did not follow Jewish dietary restrictions. To be sure, Jews did not invent the slur. We find *dogs* used pejoratively in both Euripides and Aristotle. In wrestling with this interchange between Jesus and the Canaanite woman, readers may consider the subtext and ask: What might be going on here? For instance, Angus Ritchie writes: "...perhaps his treatment of the woman is designed to draw out her inner strength, encouraging her to be bold in claiming God's blessing."[2] This is a serious attempt to make sense of Jesus' surprisingly harsh response to the woman's reasonable request. Perhaps Jesus is testing her, suggests Ritchie, probing the depth of her faith. Other interpreters have postulated that Jesus must have been smiling while responding to the woman, thus offering a non-verbal indication that he is only testing her faith. But this is only speculation. In the end, what we are left with is the text itself—the *words* on the page: "He answered, 'It is not fair to take the children's food and throw it to the dogs.' She said, 'Yes, Lord, yet even the dogs eat the crumbs that fall from their masters' table.'"

Let us be reminded here of Luke's account of Jesus in the Temple at the age of twelve (2:41-52). Luke tells us that all who heard him were "amazed" by Jesus' wisdom at such a young age. Furthermore, think about all the times when Jesus takes on Pharisees and scribes, the religious elites of the day and frequently Jesus' critics. Think about Jesus' conversation with Nicodemus in John 3. Nicodemus appears to have been a member of the Sanhedrin, the Jewish ruling council. And then there is Jesus' conversation with Pontius Pilate, the Roman territorial governor (Mt 27:11-14; Mk 15:2-5; Lk 23:2-3; Jn 18:29-38). Jesus is accustomed to having the upper hand in a disputation.

In her commentary on our passage, Margaret Davies writes of the Canaanite woman: "She is the only character in the narrative who bettered Jesus in argument."[3] *Yes, Lord, yet even the dogs eat the crumbs that fall from their masters' table*. Matthew then adds: "…Jesus answered her, 'Woman, great is your faith! Let it be done for you as you wish.' And her daughter was healed instantly." The story does, finally, have a happy ending.

It would be good to zoom out for a moment and see the forest vis-à-vis the trees. Let us think for a moment in terms of historical context. Matthew was writing late in the first century to a first-century audience. Matthew was a man *of* the first century writing *in* the first century to a first-century audience with first-century presuppositions. Amy-Jill Levine notes in *Women's Bible Commentary*: "The story of a subordinate person (foreigner, widow, poor) who begs a favor from, but is initially rebuffed by, a person in authority, but who achieves what is needed by a clever saying or action was a well-known convention."[4] Here Levine, one of our finest biblical scholars, is raising the issue of historical context, noting that *in context*, in real time, Jesus' initial response would not have been so shocking. People in the first century were accustomed to hearing stories like this, where the tenacious underdog (no pun intended) prevails. Levine makes a crucially important point for interpretation. Narratives such as this were in circulation in the first century.

Further, Matthew was writing to address a specific historical context, and in all likelihood the presenting issue for Matthew's audience was the incorporation of Gentiles into the church. The Christian movement was birthed and took shape in a Jewish cultural milieu, but as time went on it began to spread primarily among Gentiles. By the time that Matthew was writing his Gospel, ca. 70-85 AD, doubtless the church to whom he was writing was wrestling with the issue of the inclusion of Gentiles. Considering the likely historical context of Matthew's audience, this tense encounter between Jesus and the Canaanite woman proves, in the end, to be a *positive* interaction. It complements what Matthew has said in chapter 8 regarding the centurion's servant having been healed. Now, the Canaanite woman's daughter is healed. Later on we get the climactic ending of Matthew's Gospel, the Great Commission (28:16-20). Assuming an historical context concerned with the presenting issue of Gentile inclusion, this initially awkward, indeed troubling conversation between Jesus and the Canaanite woman ends in a good place. But again, in the end what we have 'in hand' is the text itself, and this initially tense exchange is troubling to a modern audience.

Let us now return to the trees. Matthew tells us that Jesus and his disciples have migrated into Gentile territory, and there they are encountered by this Canaanite woman. It is important to note that Mark, in his telling of the story, calls her a

Syrophoenician woman, a geographic reference. To call her a Syrophoenician woman focuses specifically on where she is living. But Matthew focuses more on her history. She is of Canaanite descent. Mark highlights where she is living but Matthew emphasizes her history. This is a *Canaanite* woman, and her ancestors and the ancestors of Jesus and his disciples would have been natural enemies for generations. In 2020, we would call this woman a Palestinian.

But back to Matthew. This Canaanite woman has insight. She turns to Jesus in faith, addresses him as "Lord," "Son of David," and in the face of Jesus' initial rebuff she kneels reverently, defiantly, and persists in her appeal.

In a summary comment, Amy-Jill Levine writes: "The woman then kneels before him: her position may be seen as one of humility; it can also be read as her holding her ground."[5] For this woman to have knelt before Jesus can be interpreted as a sign of submission, humility, desperation. Kneeling can connote submission, defeat, and its consequent subjugation. But, as has been made clear during social protests in recent years, kneeling can carry with it a completely different connotation. It can be a gesture of defiance. To kneel can be a way of declaring: *I'm holding my ground. I will not go away. I will not willingly yield.* The Canaanite woman had enough courage and faith to hold her ground, and to persist: *Lord, help me.* In the end she prevailed, and her daughter was healed instantly.

In his book, *Irony and Jesus: Parables, Miracles, and Stories*, Rob Gieselmann notes: "This story is the only recorded instance in Scripture in which Jesus loses an argument."[6] And she was an outsider. Amen.

CHAPTER NINETEEN

THE WORLD OF GRACE

30 August 2020 • Romans 12:9-21

[9] Let love be genuine; hate what is evil, hold fast to what is good; [10] love one another with mutual affection; outdo one another in showing honor. [11] Do not lag in zeal, be ardent in spirit, serve the Lord. [12] Rejoice in hope, be patient in suffering, persevere in prayer. [13] Contribute to the needs of the saints; extend hospitality to strangers. [14] Bless those who persecute you; bless and do not curse them. [15] Rejoice with those who rejoice, weep with those who weep. [16] Live in harmony with one another; do not be haughty, but associate with the lowly; do not claim to be wiser than you are. [17] Do not repay anyone evil for evil, but take thought for what is noble in the sight of all. [18] If it is possible, so far as it depends on you, live peaceably with all. [19] Beloved, never avenge yourselves, but leave room for the wrath of God; for it is written, "Vengeance is mine, I will repay, says the Lord." [20] No, "if your enemies are hungry, feed them; if they are thirsty, give them something to drink; for by doing this you will heap burning coals on their heads." [21] Do not be overcome by evil, but overcome evil with good.

A t this moment in our nation's history, I cannot imagine a better time to hear Romans 12:9-21 in the context of worship. This passage has much to say to us in the moment that is now.

Paul begins with: "Let love be genuine..." In the Greek of the New Testament there are several words for love, and in the era in which the New Testament documents were written the least utilized word for love was *agape*. The word does appear in extant Greek literature outside of the New Testament, but seldom. Without question, *agape* was the least utilized word for love in the Greco-Roman world prior to the Christian movement. One of the great Bible scholars of the last fifty years, James D.G. Dunn, writes on the use of *agape* in the Christian movement that Christians: "...sought to find language to express their new experience of grace, a word filled with new content and signifi-cance by earliest Christian experience of God's love."[1] The Christian experience of love was so strong that its leaders deter-mined they needed a new, a fresh term to convey their new experience of the depth of God's love in Christ. And so the Christian movement chose the existing but seldom used word *agape*, and gave it new meaning and significance. Regarding the broad sweep of New Testament documents, Dunn writes: "... love as the chief mark of Christian discipleship is strongly attested in the Synoptics and John as well as in Paul."[2] The Christian movement was grounded squarely in love: love that Jesus Christ embodied in a way previously unknown to humanity.

Paul writes in verse 9: "Let love (*agape*) be genuine..." The literal translation of the Greek would be "Let love be unhypo-critical..." The Greek word translated here as "genuine" is the word from which we get our English word "hypocrite." Dunn offers a word of caution regarding the too casual use of love (*agape*) in a Christian context. When we think of Christianity, we rightly think *love*, and yet Dunn reminds us: "...love itself can become formalized in expression, a cloak of pretense hiding an insensitive lack of genuine concern, a pretentious claim as manipulative as any coercive (pseudo-)charism, an outward form for a judgmental and condemnatory spirit."[3] We are so familiar with our Christian language of 'love' that we have to remain intentional about our *love* being genuine. Our actions must be congruent with our words.

Verse 10 begins: "...love one another with mutual affection..." The Greek here for mutual affection is *philadelphia*. When most of us were learning our American History and geography, we picked up the understanding that *Philadelphia* means "brotherly love." Philadelphia, Pennsylvania, is known as the City of Brotherly Love. This moniker comes from the Greek, *philadelphia*. Brotherly, or family love is translated in verse 10 as "mutual affection." What Paul is getting at here is the idea of family—family in the best sense of the word—a healthy family grounded in love. Paul's vision is that the Christian Church will be a loving, inclusive family. For Dunn, "This too is part of the redefinition of boundaries in which Paul engages—a sense of family belongingness which transcended immediate family ties and did not depend on natural or ethnic bonds."[4]

Let us consider Paul's vision in the context of contemporary American church culture, including the breaking down of boundaries—our evolving, more inclusive vision of a diverse *family* of believers. It is extraordinary, the relevance that Romans 12:9-21 has in the moment that is now, for those with 'eyes to see' and 'ears to hear.'

Regarding this idea of family love that Paul is urging, Dunn observes that such love "recognizes and can speak about (in the intimacy of the family) weaknesses and failings, but [it] has a quality of loyalty that outlasts repeated disappointments."[5] Here we have a vision of what family is meant to be. Of course, our personal experience of family does not always match the vision.

And when that is true for an individual parishioner, the local congregation is meant to become that person's family. I do not know how many times over the years people have said to me in a pastoral conversation: "The *church* is my family." This corresponds to the vision that Paul has here in chapter 12: Let love (*agape*), and mutual affection (*philadelphia*), be the guiding experiences in a Christian church.

In writing to the church in Rome, Paul is addressing a young Christian congregation based in a city populated with people from all over the then-known world, a city filled with mostly Gentiles, though there were Jews: people of every known race and ethnicity. We know sociologically that rich and poor together made up early Christian congregations. Though the congregation in Rome may have been relatively small, Paul was writing to as 'diverse' a population as existed in the first century. And his vision in that context is *family, mutual affection, genuine love in Christ*: everyone and everything grounded 'in Christ,' one of Paul's favorite phrases.

In verse 12 Paul writes: "Rejoice in hope, be patient in suffering, persevere in prayer." The New English Bible translates verse 12: "Let hope keep you joyful; in trouble stand firm; persist in prayer." I offer this translation to you as we face our many challenges. Between the pandemic and widespread social protests, we are living in a perfect storm of challenges, but in these challenges also lie opportunity and hope. *Let hope keep you joyful; in trouble stand firm; persist in prayer.*

The word for hope in biblical Greek connotes a *tentative expectation*. But in biblical Hebrew the word for hope implies *confident trust*. Paul was as cosmopolitan a person as was possible in the first century. He would have been fluent both in Greek and in the Hebrew of his religious heritage, and in verse 12 Paul doubtless has the Hebrew connotation in mind—hope grounded in *confident trust* that God is always with us, and that God's love, grace, and strength will carry us through whatever challenges we face.

"Rejoice in hope..." "Let hope keep you joyful..." Verse 12 is not a platitude. This is not escapist spiritual rhetoric. By this point in his missionary career, Paul has lived a very full life. Romans is the fruit of a mature mind. Paul is urging his hearers to have a meaningfully confident *trust* in the love of God shown to us most fully in Jesus Christ.

Our passage concludes: "Do not be overcome by evil, but overcome evil with good." This admonition is grounded in the cross. There is no doubt here that Paul has the cross in mind, where the depth of the love of Jesus is shown most fully. In his commentary on our passage, N.T. Wright observes: "...when human evil reached its height God came and took its full weight upon himself, thereby exhausting it and opening the way for the creation of a new world altogether."[6] The new world that the cross and resurrection open up is the world of grace, the world of forgiveness and reconciliation—the world of hope—that the risen Christ offers at every moment. This new reality, this new experience of love is what inspired Christians to find a new word to convey what they were experiencing—*agape*.

Elsewhere, Wright notes regarding verse 21: "This is the theology of the cross at work in the world."[7] *Do not be overcome by evil, but overcome evil with good.* Dunn comments on verse 21: "Christ's answer to evil is always and never other than a positive act of good."[8] How timely an observation for us in our perfect storm of challenge, this ancient wisdom from Christianity's great early apostle to the diverse Greco-Roman world. For Paul, Christ's answer to evil is *always and never other than a positive act of good.*

During this tension-filled season, I am continually reminded of an insight of Karl Barth (1886-1968), one of the great biblical theologians of the twentieth century. Barth observed that in preparing a sermon, a preacher should have the Bible in one hand and a newspaper in the other. In thinking this past week about our passage containing Paul's extraordinary vision of what a loving Christian community can be, I could not get out of my mind the words of a contemporary visionary, Julia Jackson, the mother of Jacob Blake. In a prophetic, visionary statement this past week, Julia Jackson said: "We need healing. As I pray for my son's healing—physically, emotionally and spiritually—I also have been praying, even before this for the healing of our country."[9] And then in a plea to Americans of every race and background, Julia Jackson said: "Let's use our hearts, our love and our intelligence to work together to show the rest of the world how humans are supposed to treat each other."[10] Amen.

CHAPTER TWENTY
A LOVE THAT IS NOT EASY

6 September 2020 • Romans 13:8-14

[8] Owe no one anything, except to love one another; for the one who loves another has fulfilled the law. [9] The commandments, "You shall not commit adultery; You shall not murder; You shall not steal; You shall not covet"; and any other commandment, are summed up in this word, "Love your neighbor as yourself." [10] Love does no wrong to a neighbor; therefore, love is the fulfilling of the law. [11] Besides this, you know what time it is, how it is now the moment for you to wake from sleep. For salvation is nearer to us now than when we became believers; [12] the night is far gone, the day is near. Let us then lay aside the works of darkness and put on the armor of light; [13] let us live honorably as in the day, not in reveling and drunkenness, not in debauchery and licentiousness, not in quarreling and jealousy. [14] Instead, put on the Lord Jesus Christ, and make no provision for the flesh, to gratify its desires.

Romans 13:8-10 is an exceptionally important passage in considering Paul's understanding of the relationship between law and grace. In verse 9, "'Love your neighbor as yourself'" is a quotation from Leviticus 19:18. The commandment is of obvious importance to Jesus, as he invokes it on numerous occasions. In Matthew 22:37-40 we read: "[Jesus said] 'You shall love the Lord your God with all your heart, and with all your soul, and with all your mind.' This is the greatest and first commandment. And a second is like it: 'You shall love your neighbor as yourself.' On these two commandments hang all the law and the prophets."

Love your neighbor as yourself. In his commentary on Romans 13:8-14, N.T. Wright observes: "The point of love, genuine Christian love, what the New Testament writers call *agapē*...was that it meant copying the self-giving love of Jesus himself."[1] Earlier in Romans, Paul writes in 12:9: "Let love be genuine..." The more literal translation is: "Let love be unhypocritical." Here Paul is calling us to a sacrificial love, a love that is not easy —love modeled on that of Christ himself.

Paul then writes in 13:14: "put on the Lord Jesus Christ..." Here we have a reference to baptism, when we 'put on' Christ. In his commentary, David M. Kasali writes: "We need to consciously and constantly put on Christ, that is, decide to live under his lordship and allow Christ to control all aspects of our lives."[2] I am particularly struck by the introduction to Kasali's comments: *We need to consciously and constantly...* Moment by moment, day by day, we need consciously and constantly to *put on Christ* in order to love as he would have us love.

Owe no one anything, except to love one another; for the one who loves another has fulfilled the law (13:8). It sounds wonderful, does it not? Clear, concise, and yet what we are being asked to do is to make a radical commitment. Some people make it easy to love them, and there is no sacrifice involved in such love. Others we find much harder to love. In Romans 13:8-10 there are no qualifiers, no limitations. There is no 'out clause.' We are to love one another when it comes easily and naturally, effortlessly, *and* when it is difficult and deeply challenging. In all circumstances, however challenging, we are meant to remember, and be guided by, Jesus' command to love.

Let us recall the parable of the Good Samaritan (Lk 10:25-37). In verse 29, a lawyer in conversation with Jesus asks him: "'And who is my neighbor?'" The lawyer is looking for qualifiers. He is looking for limitations to the commandment. The lawyer is looking for an out clause. *Who* is my neighbor? How can I limit the scope, the *reach* of the commandment? But Jesus will have none of it, and goes on to offer one of his most memorable teachings.

We are to love our neighbor—no matter where he comes from. We are to love our neighbor—regardless of how long she has been here, or how long she plans to stay.

Some of the best advice I have ever heard regarding preaching is: "Preach *to* yourself, not *of* yourself." These words are instructive, haunting, and humbling. Preach *to* yourself, not *of* yourself. The commandment to love your neighbor—regardless—is as hard for me as it is for you. I can get my back up with the best of them when something or someone rubs me the wrong way. Nevertheless, the commandment to love our neighbor is in Leviticus. It runs all through the teachings of Jesus. And Paul addresses it squarely. *Love your neighbor as yourself* is also prominent in our Baptismal Covenant. At every baptism, as we welcome another sister or brother into the household of God, we renew our Baptismal Covenant, and there comes that point when the officiant asks: "Will you proclaim by word and example the Good News of God in Christ?" *I will, with God's help.* "Will you seek and serve Christ in all persons, loving your neighbor as yourself?" *I will, with God's help.* "Will you strive for justice and peace among all people, and respect the dignity of every human being?" *I will, with God's help.*[3] No qualifiers. No limitations. No out clause.

Returning for just a moment to Luke 10, in concluding the parable of the Good Samaritan Jesus says to the lawyer (v. 36): "Which of these...was a neighbor to the man who fell into the hands of the robbers?" The lawyer responds (v. 37): "The one who showed him mercy." In view of the historical setting of the parable, we can readily imagine the lawyer choking on the words, as it is the Samaritan who proves to be the exemplar—a foreigner, the 'other.' Then Jesus says to him: "Go and do likewise."

For my birthday in 1991, two dear parishioners in St. Andrew's Church, Canton, North Carolina, gave me a lovely little devotional book called *A Common Prayer. A Common Prayer* is a compilation of illustrated prayers by Michael Leunig. I keep the book in a prominent place in my study at home and pull it from the shelf frequently to remind myself of its concise, simple teachings: simple in terms of clarity, though oftentimes much easier said than done. It is a wonderful devotional book. At the end of the book, its final prayer sums up everything that Leunig has been trying to say from page one through to the end: "'Love one another, and you will be happy.' It's as simple and as difficult as that. There is no other way."[4] Amen.

CHAPTER TWENTY-ONE

AN EXTRAORDINARY PORTRAIT OF GRACE

13 September 2020 • *Genesis 50:15-21*

[15] Realizing that their father was dead, Joseph's brothers said, "What if Joseph still bears a grudge against us and pays us back in full for all the wrong that we did to him?" [16] So they approached Joseph, saying, "Your father gave this instruction before he died, [17] 'Say to Joseph: I beg you, forgive the crime of your brothers and the wrong they did in harming you.' Now therefore please forgive the crime of the servants of the God of your father." Joseph wept when they spoke to him. [18] Then his brothers also wept, fell down before him, and said, "We are here as your slaves." [19] But Joseph said to them, "Do not be afraid! Am I in the place of God? [20] Even though you intended to do harm to me, God intended it for good, in order to preserve a numerous people, as he is doing today. [21] So have no fear; I myself will provide for you and your little ones." In this way he reassured them, speaking kindly to them.

The saga of Joseph and his brothers in the book of Genesis is practically a novella. The saga begins in chapter 37 and runs through to the end of Genesis in chapter 50. Joel W. Rosenberg has said of the Joseph story that it is a "magisterial saga."[1] Gerhard von Rad has written that the saga of Joseph and his brothers is "a wide-ranging work of art..."[2] Storytelling, ancient or contemporary, does not get any better than the story of Joseph and his brothers. The author who has crafted the Joseph saga into its final form is clearly "a literary artist of refined imagination."[3] The epic tale of Joseph and his brothers reads as compellingly—and is as full of meaning—today as it was when first written.

When we first meet Joseph (Genesis 37) he is privileged. He is arrogant. He has been spoiled and it shows, so much so that his own brothers want to kill him. And then they have the idea: We could make money by selling him into slavery. Such was the hatred that his brothers had come to have for Joseph.

Joseph goes from being a spoiled brat to being a slave in a foreign land. Like a lot of great sagas, this one is about arrogance giving way to humility. Life has a way of reducing us to our proper size. You probably know the truism: Sometimes you're the windshield, sometimes you're the bug. In the minor leagues of professional baseball there is a saying: Be nice to people on your way up because you'll see them again on your way down.

In the end, Joseph *is* special. John Sanford, an Episcopal priest and Jungian analyst, has written: "Certain individuals are called upon to achieve a greatly accentuated consciousness and highly developed personality."[4] In Egypt, Joseph rises from being a slave to becoming the second highest ranking person in the kingdom, second only to Pharaoh. Gerhard von Rad notes of Joseph's Egypt years that he rises from "...deepest misery to highest honor."[5] He continues: "One does not, of course, attain such a model life as shown by Joseph overnight. One must first learn it in the difficult school of humility."⁶

Over the course of a lifetime, some of us find ourselves being re-enrolled periodically in the difficult school of humility- I do not think that we ever really graduate! Like most good sagas, the Joseph story contains a reversal, a major plot twist. In the saga, the brothers, who start out as the windshield, become the bug. When we pick up the story in Genesis 50:15-21, Jacob, the great patriarch, has died. There is a famine in the brothers' homeland, and they are in a state of desperation. Genesis tells us that they "fell down before [Joseph]." They prostrated themselves. They were groveling. In 50:18 we see the brothers say to Joseph: "We are here as your slaves." What we see here is a complete reversal of roles, and we are reminded of the prodigal son. In a foreign land the prodigal comes to realize: My father's servants have it better than I do. Luke tells us in 15:19 that the prodigal prepares himself to address his father: "I am no longer worthy to be called your son; treat me like one of your hired hands." He is prepared to go home to his father having forfeited his sonship, hoping only to receive some level of mercy.

In *Africa Bible Commentary*, the commentators on Genesis write: "There are many people who look for forgiveness without really accepting the depths of their failure."⁷ Have you ever had anyone expect you to forgive them, and you realize that they have not really apologized? There are people who look for forgiveness without really acknowledging their 'sin.' That is not the case in this saga. The brothers know that they mistreated Joseph horribly. They know the depth of their sin. Likewise, in Luke, the prodigal understands how wrong he was to leave his father's house. Joseph's brothers *are* repentant, as is the prodigal. Imagine the brothers being forced into the position of prostrating themselves and saying to Joseph whom they had sold into slavery: "We are here as your slaves."

In 50:19 we read: "But Joseph said to them, 'Do not be

afraid! Am I in the place of God?'" Here we find one of the great moments of grace in all of literature, certainly in all of Scripture. Joseph himself has had the experience of being humbled. He knows what it is like to be a slave. When he has every opportunity to get back at his brothers, he is kind to them instead: *Do not be afraid! Am I in the place of God?* We see here an extraordinary portrait of grace. Let us remember the father in the Parable of the Prodigal Son. The son has renounced his father and everything his father stands for. He goes away to a foreign land but realizes in the end what a terrible mistake he has made. If you will remember, in the parable Luke tells us that the father stays on the lookout for his son's return. On that fateful day of the son's return, when the prodigal is still at a distance the father sees him and runs to embrace him. When the son tries to say: *If you will just let me be your servant, that will be enough,* the father will have none of it. He throws his arms around him and makes it absolutely clear: You are my *son*, and I love you.

Joseph forgives his brothers. Where does such grace come from? How can Joseph find it in his heart to be so merciful, so conciliatory, so gracious—so deeply compassionate? And, how can we? When we have been aggrieved, when something unjust has happened to us—how do we find the grace to forgive? How do we find it within ourselves to be gracious, merciful, and compassionate? Can we find within ourselves the grace to forgive as we have been forgiven?

In his commentary on the Joseph saga, Angus Ritchie writes: "Our forgiveness of others is not a matter of obedience to an external command, but an expression of the divine life within us."[8] A powerful insight. Every time we have a baptism in the Episcopal Church we renew our Baptismal Covenant. In the lead-up to each baptism we renew our own baptismal promises, our own baptismal commitments. Every time we make a promise in the Covenant, we do so with the words: "I will, with

God's help." *I will seek and serve Christ in all persons. I will respect the dignity of every human being.* "I will, with God's help."[9]

The author of the Epistle of James puts it so crisply, so clearly, and so memorably in 5:11: "the Lord is compassionate and merciful." Among the Gospel writers, Luke is the most intentional about portraying God as compassionate and merciful. It is only in Luke 6:36 that we read these exact words: "Be merciful, just as your Father is merciful." The Greek for "merciful" can also be translated as "compassionate." The verse can be translated: "Be compassionate, just as your Father is compassionate." Our forgiveness of others is not merely a matter of obedience to an external command, but an expression of the divine life within us. Which, in the end, is another way of saying: Let go, and let God. Amen.

CHAPTER TWENTY-TWO

THE WIDENESS OF GOD'S MERCY

20 September 2020 • Matthew 20:1-16

[1] Jesus said, "For the kingdom of heaven is like a landowner who went out early in the morning to hire laborers for his vineyard. [2] After agreeing with the laborers for the usual daily wage, he sent them into his vineyard. [3] When he went out about nine o'clock, he saw others standing idle in the marketplace; [4] and he said to them, 'You also go into the vineyard, and I will pay you whatever is right.' So they went. [5] When he went out again about noon and about three o'clock, he did the same. [6] And about five o'clock he went out and found others standing around; and he said to them, 'Why are you standing here idle all day?' [7] They said to him, 'Because no one has hired us.' He said to them, 'You also go into the vineyard.' [8] When evening came, the owner of the vineyard said to his manager, 'Call the laborers and give them their pay, beginning with the last and then going to the first.' [9] When those hired about five o'clock came, each of them received the usual daily wage. [10] Now when the first came, they thought they would receive more; but each of them also

received the usual daily wage. [11] And when they received it, they grumbled against the landowner, [12] saying, 'These last worked only one hour, and you have made them equal to us who have borne the burden of the day and the scorching heat.' [13] But he replied to one of them, 'Friend, I am doing you no wrong; did you not agree with me for the usual daily wage? [14] Take what belongs to you and go; I choose to give to this last the same as I give to you. [15] Am I not allowed to do what I choose with what belongs to me? Or are you envious because I am generous?' [16] So the last will be first, and the first will be last."

The first parish I served as an ordained minister was St. Andrew's Episcopal Church in Canton, North Carolina. The first person from Canton I ever heard from was Carroll Waldroop, chairman of the search committee. He called early one Saturday morning while I was still in seminary. And it was early! Carroll did not realize that Sewanee is on Central Time. He was calling to invite me to come and interview to be the pastor of St. Andrew's. I was twenty-seven years old, the youngest student in the seminary. To this day I can remember the drive over to Canton for the interview on a Saturday, and then the 'trial sermon' on Sunday morning. The closer I got to the Canton exit the more nervous I became, so much so that in nearing Canton, a part of me wished that I was getting *farther away* as the nervous tension mounted. But in the end, it all worked out really well, and I remain grateful to the people of St. Andrew's to this day.

Carroll Waldroop was the senior electrician at Champion Papers, the biggest employer in town. He was a union man, and he had worked as an employee advocate his entire career. He was the Junior Warden (responsible for oversight of the church property) at St. Andrew's for most of my tenure, and he was from central casting in that role. Carroll could fix 'anything,' and if he could not fix it he knew someone who could. He was a hardworking, good man.

His new pastor was young and inexperienced, and yet Carroll always knew that my heart was in the right place, and he was wonderfully supportive. I do not remember there ever being a cross word between us. All these years later I can remember one particular Sunday in Canton when I preached on Matthew 20:1-16, the Parable of the Laborers in the Vineyard. On his way out of church that Sunday, Carroll looked me in the eye, took my hand into his, and said: "I liked everything you had to say in your sermon." Words every preacher loves to hear. And then he took my hand a little firmer, leaned in a little closer where only I could hear, and said: "But those men who worked more hours should have gotten paid more!"

Of course, at one level he was right. But then again, this story is not really about economics. In the end, this is not a story about employer/employee relations. In his commentary on the Gospel of Matthew, Craig Blomberg writes regarding 20:1-16: "The significance of this parable can scarcely be overestimated."[1] This is because it offers such a memorable and instructive portrait of God's grace. In *Interpreting the Parables*, A.M. Hunter writes of our passage that it is "one of the most beautiful—and disconcerting—of all the parables because it most arrestingly proclaims the grace of the God who brings the kingdom..."[2] A wise observation. I particularly appreciate Hunter's use of the words *disconcerting* and *arrestingly*. We cannot miss the point. This parable is unmistakably about the radical nature of God's grace. To me the Parable of the Laborers in the Vineyard is on the level of the Parable of the Prodigal Son, both of which disconcertingly and arrestingly proclaim the reckless mercy of God's abiding love.

In the end, this story is not about labor relations. It is not about fair wages in the marketplace. In the end, it is not even about work. It is about grace. The Parable of the Laborers in the

Vineyard proclaims the extravagance of the depths of God's love for *all* in the human family. Hunter further observes: "...God's love cannot be portioned out in quantities nicely adjusted to the merits of individuals."[3] An important observation. God does not measure out mercy based on our merit. God's grace is poured out equally to all.

Of course, the laborers in the story who had worked all day in the hot sun grumbled when they saw what was happening at the end of the day. But the key point in the parable really is verse 15, when the landowner says: "Am I not allowed to do what I choose with what belongs to me? Or are you envious because I am generous?" Here the wideness of God's mercy is framed unmistakably clearly. It is God's *choice* to be generous to all.

C.S. Lewis once observed that *the* most widespread and chronic temptation is the desire for a better seat at the table. Here Lewis is referring to envy. About the landowner in the parable, Stephen Wright observes: "...he is not acting to deprive the first workers but to be generous towards the later ones."[4] The landowner gives to all the workers everything that they have been promised, including those who arrive at the end of the day and have only worked a short while. The takeaway here is that as long as we have breath, there exists the opportunity for us to turn and receive God's loving kindness—*grace*—in abundance.

I am deeply blessed to have had a wonderful father-in-law. Fred Williams was gracious to me from the day we met and was extraordinarily generous in welcoming me into the family. He was a wonderful man, and I miss him to this day. In reflecting on our passage, I remember that every time my father-in-law said the blessing over a meal, and every time he prayed an invocation at a family gathering, his first prayerful words were: "Father, thank you for your kindness." A moving interpretation and application of the Parable of the Laborers in the Vineyard.

John Claypool was a prominent and highly respected Southern Baptist pastor and preacher. Relatively late in his career, Claypool switched denominations and became an Episcopal priest. I have said for years that ex-Southern Baptists can make great Episcopalians! In his book on the parables, *Stories Jesus Still Tells*, Claypool writes about verse 15: "'Am I not free to do with my abundance what I want? Or do you begrudge me my generosity?' Deeper than the issues of justice or fairness, this is the pivotal point of the whole story."[5] Claypool goes on to observe: "a fail-safe recipe for joy is regarding our life as a gift. A fail-safe recipe for misery is comparing our lot to someone else's and forgetting what a grace life really is."[6] A potentially life-changing insight. And he continues: "every one of the workers had an occasion for gratitude if they had only remembered what their circumstances were like before dawn."[7] The landowner kept every promise that he had made, and, in the end, was generous to all.

Matthew 20:1-16 is one of the most *beautiful* and *disconcerting* of all the parables because it *most arrestingly* proclaims the grace, mercy, and generosity of God. In reflecting on the Parable of the Laborers in the Vineyard, I am reminded of another "arresting" theological statement. Many years ago I was reading a book by Br. David Steindl-Rast called *Gratefulness, the Heart of Prayer: An Approach to Life in Fullness*. The book contains an arresting one-liner which conveys a perfect interpretation of the Parable of the Laborers in the Vineyard. I find it hauntingly instructive. The line is this: "everything is gratuitous, everything is gift."[8] Amen.

CHAPTER TWENTY-THREE

GOTTA SERVE SOMEBODY

27 September 2020 • Philippians 2:1-13

[1] If then there is any encouragement in Christ, any consolation from love, any sharing in the Spirit, any compassion and sympathy, [2] make my joy complete: be of the same mind, having the same love, being in full accord and of one mind. [3] Do nothing from selfish ambition or conceit, but in humility regard others as better than yourselves. [4] Let each of you look not to your own interests, but to the interests of others. [5] Let the same mind be in you that was in Christ Jesus, [6] who, though he was in the form of God, did not regard equality with God as something to be exploited, [7] but emptied himself, taking the form of a slave, being born in human likeness. And being found in human form, [8] he humbled himself and became obedient to the point of death—even death on a cross. [9] Therefore God also highly exalted him and gave him the name that is above every name, [10] so that at the name of Jesus every knee should bend, in heaven and on earth and under the earth, [11] and every tongue should confess that Jesus Christ is Lord, to the glory of God the Father. [12] Therefore, my beloved, just as you have always obeyed

me, not only in my presence, but much more now in my absence, work out your own salvation with fear and trembling; [13] for it is God who is at work in you, enabling you both to will and to work for his good pleasure.

One of my favorite spiritual authors is Henri Nouwen. I am not alone in my appreciation of Nouwen. By some metrics Nouwen was, at least at one point, the most widely read Christian writer in the world. My devotion to him is shared by countless others. Henri Nouwen died unexpectedly from a heart attack in 1996.

I remember where I was when I got the news that Nouwen had died. I was in my office, and read in *The Living Church* the shocking news of Nouwen's passing. I can remember to this day my feelings of sadness and disbelief that one of our great spiritual writers had left us so suddenly.

Nouwen's best book by his own estimation, and in the estimation of many of his readers, is *The Return of the Prodigal Son: A Story of Homecoming*. Nouwen was quite open about the fact that he regarded the prodigal son book as his best. It is his best-selling book and is a classic of Christian spirituality. Italo Calvino, a journalist and writer of short stories, in *The Uses of Literature* writes: "A classic is a book that has never finished saying what it has to say."[1] A great definition of a *classic*, be it a book, a movie, a play, or a piece of music: *A classic...has never finished saying what it has to say*.

Gabrielle Earnshaw is an authority on the life and work of Henri Nouwen, and she has written a book about *The Return of the Prodigal Son* called: *Henri Nouwen & The Return of the Prodigal Son*. She writes of Nouwen's classic: "It is...one of those rare books that reveals something new with each reading. Perhaps this is the true criterion of a spiritual classic: like Scripture it changes with each reading. As we mature, more is revealed."[2]

Philippians 2:1-13 is one of the great passages in all of Scripture. At the heart of the passage is the Christ Hymn, verses 5-11. The *Christ Hymn*, we think, is an actual hymn from the first century. Most scholars think that it may well be the earliest known piece of Christian liturgy, and thus we are on holy ground when we hear and seek to interpret the Christ Hymn. In encountering the Christ Hymn we are in contact with the first generation of Christians.

N.T. Wright says of our passage that it is: "one of the noblest early Christian statements of Jesus' person and accomplishment..."[3] Wright also notes: "subsequent theology has gazed at [it] in awe for its remarkably full and rich statement of what was later seen as the classic doctrine of the incarnation of God in Jesus the Messiah."[4] Subsequent Christian apologists have not done better in stating succinctly who Jesus is. Two thousand years of theological reflection has not improved upon the Christ Hymn.

In 1979, Bob Dylan came out with an album, *Slow Train Coming*, which included the single, "Gotta Serve Somebody." I listened to the song as part of my preparation for this address. "Gotta Serve Somebody" was Bob Dylan's last Top 40 hit. Dylan was awarded that year's Grammy for Best Rock Vocal Performance. *Gotta Serve Somebody*. The Christ Hymn conveys succinctly and movingly that we are to serve Christ as he came to serve us.

Let the same mind be in you that was in Christ Jesus, who, though he was in the form of God, did not regard equality with God as something to be exploited, but emptied himself, taking the form of a slave, being born in human likeness [incarnation]. And being found in human form, he humbled himself and became obedient to the point of death—even death on a cross [crucifixion]. Therefore God also highly exalted him [resurrection] and gave him the name that is above every name, so that at the name of Jesus every knee should bend [Gotta Serve

Somebody], in heaven and on earth and under the earth, and every tongue should confess that Jesus Christ is Lord, to the glory of God the Father.

Fred Craddock has a wonderfully dynamic translation of verses 5-8 of the Christ Hymn: "I want you to have the mind of Jesus Christ who did not count being equal with God something to be clutched. But he turned it loose and emptied himself and became a servant and a human being. And being in human form he was obedient unto death, the death on the cross."[5] He did not *clutch* equality with God, but gave it up, *turned it loose* to come and live among us and show us the way.

The Christ Hymn is sometimes called the Kenotic Hymn, from the Greek word *kenosis* which means to empty. He *emptied* himself... Jesus Christ is our model of a healthy humility. In the Old Testament there is a long line of teaching about the virtue of humility. But in the Greco-Roman world, of which Philippi was a part, humility was not seen as a virtue. In the Greek of the period the word for humility had a connotation of servility and weakness. Until the spread of Christianity, to be humble in the Greco-Roman world meant to be weak. Ralph P. Martin writes: "It was apparently through the teaching of Jesus that humility came to be regarded as a virtue."[6] And Richard R. Melick, Jr., notes: "Christ's humility is the standard for evaluating the worth of others and actions toward them."[7] Paul puts it: "Let the same mind be in you that was in Christ Jesus..." Have humility like that of Jesus. Have a servant's heart like that of Jesus. Imagine a culture wherein humility is seen only as weakness, and then the teaching of one person changes the whole tenor of the conversation. That person was Jesus. Jesus' humility becomes *the* standard for our evaluation of the worth of others and our actions toward them. When we contemplate our experience of someone else, or our action toward them, the question for us to ask is: *What would Jesus do?* Who is this person in the eyes of Jesus?

This past Thursday night I was headed home from the YMCA and all was well until someone suddenly needed to change lanes and cut right in front of me. If I had not been using my best defensive driving principles, we would have collided. Out of nowhere, he cut right in front of me. After the collision had been avoided, I noticed the rear window sticker of his car, which read: "Honk If You Love Jesus!" If I had honked in that moment, it would not have been because I love Jesus!

In addition to Henri Nouwen, one of my favorite spiritual writers is Frederick Buechner. One of the books written in response to Buechner's work is Jeffrey Munroe's *Reading Buechner: Exploring the Work of a Master Memoirist, Novelist, Theologian, and Preacher.* In the context of reflecting on Buechner's activities during the 1960s, Munroe writes: "America erupted in the late 1960s..."[8] That phrase really catches my attention in 2020— America *erupted* in the late 1960s.

Well, it is erupting again. We in this country know what a reference to the late 1960s means—anger at systemic injustices boiling over into violence, accompanied by demands for meaningful and lasting systemic change. And from now on, we will know what we mean when we refer to 2020. America is erupting again, and, at some level, each of us has to ask the question of ourselves: What is my response? How do I respond in this defining cultural moment? We do well to frame our response by looking to the person and teachings of Jesus.

I leave us not with my words, nor even the words of Bob Dylan, but with Paul. In this tense cultural moment, those of us who follow Jesus are not without guidance. We have been given timeless, guiding principles, and of all times now is the moment for us to be at our best as followers of the Christ. *Let the same mind be in you that was in Christ Jesus...* Amen.

CHAPTER TWENTY-FOUR
A LIVING TEXT

25 October 2020 • 1 Thessalonians 2:1-8

[1] You yourselves know, brothers and sisters, that our coming to you was not in vain, [2] but though we had already suffered and been shamefully mistreated at Philippi, as you know, we had courage in our God to declare to you the gospel of God in spite of great opposition. [3] For our appeal does not spring from deceit or impure motives or trickery, [4] but just as we have been approved by God to be entrusted with the message of the gospel, even so we speak, not to please mortals, but to please God who tests our hearts. [5] As you know and as God is our witness, we never came with words of flattery or with a pretext for greed; [6] nor did we seek praise from mortals, whether from you or from others, [7] though we might have made demands as apostles of Christ. But we were gentle among you, like a nurse tenderly caring for her own children. [8] So deeply do we care for you that we are determined to share with you not only the gospel of God but also our own selves, because you have become very dear to us.

B efore Michael Mayne became Dean of Westminster Abbey in 1986, he was Vicar of Great St. Mary's Church (The University Church), Cambridge, founded in 1209 by the university to serve the university community. Mayne served Great St. Mary's from 1979-1986. While there, he carried on the tradition of inviting top guest speakers to address the church, the university, and the wider community. Many of these events took place at 8:00 pm on Sunday evenings, which may seem a little late to most of us, but in a university setting during term, 8:00 pm makes perfect sense. As one might imagine, Mayne was able to bring to Great St. Mary's just about any speaker he wanted in the field of spirituality. Years later, Mayne —having served as host of these events—reflected on something that happened frequently with these noted guests brought in to speak to the Cambridge community. It was typical for speakers to ask him: Do you have any advice? Bear in mind, these were well-known, experienced people who made their living speaking and writing. Mayne's advice was this: "If it is in your nature to do so, be vulnerable. Don't be afraid to talk about yourself, *your* journey, *your* pain, *your* vision."[1] In other words: *Be yourself. Be authentic.* Michael Mayne had the pastoral wisdom to know that the audience would connect with a speaker who was willing to be vulnerable, to speak personally from the heart. Mayne knew that, whatever the speaker might ultimately say, it was the speaker's bearing that the audience would remember, his or her authenticity.

Biblical scholars think that 1 Thessalonians is the oldest book in the New Testament, safely dated to 50-51 AD. Of course, the Gospels and Acts refer to earlier history, but regarding the New Testament documents themselves, 1 Thessalonians is widely held to be the oldest book in the New Testament canon. Paul, along with his ministry colleagues Silvanus and Timothy, founded the church in Thessalonica. We can read about that in Acts 17:1-10, which is not a boring passage! Acts 17 contains some crucial early Christian history. In 1 Thessalonians 2:2 Paul writes to the congregation: "...we had courage in our God to declare to you the gospel of God in spite of great opposition." Notice that Paul uses "we," not "I." Paul values the contributions of his colleagues. He writes further: "For our appeal does not spring from deceit or impure motives or trickery..." Again, "our" appeal, not "my" appeal. Paul clearly understood the value of team ministry.

1 Thessalonians takes on a warm, pastoral tone. It is clear from the outset that Paul loves his audience and they love him. When pastor and people are in sync, it is a beautiful thing, and we get a glimpse of that in 1 Thessalonians. In 2:7 Paul writes: "But we were *gentle* (emphasis mine) among you, like a nurse tenderly caring for her own children." The word for "nurse" here in Greek is *trophos*. *Trophos* means "nursing mother." It can also mean "wet nurse."

Paul uses similar language in Galatians 4:19: "My little children, for whom I am again in the pain of childbirth until Christ is formed in you..." This is extraordinary language for a first-century alpha male to use. Both in Galatians and in 1 Thessalonians, Paul is comfortable employing feminine imagery to convey the depths of Christian love. D. Michael Martin writes in his commentary on 2:1-8: "Paul's work was not carried out with detached professionalism."[2] Paul is deeply involved in the lives of the church community in Thessalonica.

We have had a number of funerals in our church during the pandemic. One of those was for John Simmons. On the day of John's service, which was private because of our COVID protocols, his daughter Kim spoke, as did her daughter Michaela. In these family remarks something was said that I did not anticipate, and which really caught my attention. In remembering her father, Kim said of John—a quiet, reserved yet alpha male if there ever was one—that he had observed: "God must have a lot of woman in him because he is so forgiving." I was struck by two things in that moment. First of all, I did not know that John Simmons had ever said that. And, second, I would never have expected him to have said that! But he had. *God must have a lot of woman in him because he is so forgiving.*

Paul uses feminine imagery to convey the depth of love that Christians are to have for one another. Writing in *Women's Bible Commentary*, Monya Stubbs observes that scholars estimate that in the first-century biblical world the infant mortality rate was about thirty percent.[3] Let that number sink in. It is estimated that in Paul's world the infant mortality rate was *thirty percent*. It is in that historical context that his words take on their deepest meaning: *But we were gentle among you, like a nurse tenderly caring for her own children.* D. Michael Martin notes: "A gospel messenger who stands detached from his audience has not yet been touched by the very gospel he proclaims. The Gospel creates a community characterized by love."[4]

1 Thessalonians 2:8: "So deeply do we care for you that we are determined to share with you not only the gospel of God but also our own selves, because you have become very dear to us." Here we get back to Michael Mayne. To the prominent, in many cases internationally known guest speakers brought in to speak to the university community of Cambridge, Mayne's advice to them was: *If it is in your nature to do so, be vulnerable. Be yourself. Be authentic.* In the end, the reality is that we forget the vast majority of the words we hear. As a speaker, I am aware that you will forget most of what I say. What we remember are first impressions. We remember what 'hits us in the gut.' We remember the lasting impression that we get from people. Was he believable? Did she seem sincere? Were they *real*? That is the relationship that Paul, Silvanus, and Timothy have with the church in Thessalonica. Paul makes it clear: We are not just sharing the Gospel with you. We are sharing ourselves.

1 Thessalonians is not Paul's best-known epistle. When we

think of Paul's letters we may instinctively think of Romans, or 1 Corinthians, or perhaps Ephesians. That said, 1 Thessalonians is the oldest book in the New Testament and provides us an invaluable glimpse into an early Christian community—an example of what scholars call "primitive Christianity." 1 Thessalonians 2:1-8 gives us a glimpse into an early Christian congregation, and what we take away from the passage is the importance of community. The importance of authenticity. The importance of trustworthiness. All of which is dependent upon the foundation of love for one another.

In 2020, in St. Luke's and in all Christian congregations, *community* is crucially important. St. Luke's is a tight-knit community, and as we work through this pandemic and eventually emerge from it, it is crucial that we hold onto the importance of community. As we endure this pandemic and, in time, move beyond it, our familiar, *traditional* sense of community will remain as important as ever, and yet—with the advent of live-streaming—the pandemic presents us and every Christian congregation with opportunities to reimagine what community *can be*. The pandemic presents to us the occasion, indeed, the necessity, of redefining our traditional sense of boundaries. Live-streaming is now simply a part of church life going forward. This practice started as a practical necessity. Churches had to do *something* to offer parishioners access to communal worship. But over time, churches have begun to realize the enormous opportunities that live-streamed worship, education, and other offerings present for pastoral care in the broadest sense of that term.

Amidst the pandemic we have come to realize that live-streaming is an extraordinary platform for evangelism. In reality, churches can now offer pastoral care to a nearly limitless potential audience. There are now few inherent limits regarding who can avail themselves of the ministries of churches with online platforms. An irony of this difficult season is that new opportunities for ministry have blossomed, and churches now have more ways than ever before to offer connectivity and community to an audience no longer limited by geography. We now have more opportunities to proclaim in accessible, authentic, and compelling ways the love and the grace of Jesus Christ. That said, technology can and will only do so much. In the end, the technology is a tool, a platform, a vehicle; yet, what matters most is the message—the accessible, authentic, trustworthy message of love, forgiveness, grace, and healing. Technology now gives churches the opportunity to reach beyond their 'four walls,' but once the platform is in place it is the *message* that matters. In commenting on 1 Thessalonians 2:1-8, Angus Ritchie writes: "Each disciple, in proclaiming the Gospel, must become a 'living text.'"[5] Amen.

CHAPTER TWENTY-FIVE

THE JOYFUL SERVICE OF THOSE IN NEED

All Saints' Day
1 November 2020 • Matthew 5:1-12

[1] When Jesus saw the crowds, he went up the mountain; and after he sat down, his disciples came to him. [2] Then he began to speak, and taught them, saying: [3] "Blessed are the poor in spirit, for theirs is the kingdom of heaven. [4] Blessed are those who mourn, for they will be comforted. [5] Blessed are the meek, for they will inherit the earth. [6] Blessed are those who hunger and thirst for righteousness, for they will be filled. [7] Blessed are the merciful, for they will receive mercy. [8] Blessed are the pure in heart, for they will see God. [9] Blessed are the peacemakers, for they will be called children of God. [10] Blessed are those who are persecuted for righteousness' sake, for theirs is the kingdom of heaven. [11] Blessed are you when people revile you and persecute you and utter all kinds of evil against you falsely on my account. [12] Rejoice and be glad, for your reward is great in heaven, for in the same way they persecuted the prophets who were before you."

The American lecturer, poet, essayist and leading exponent of New England Transcendentalism, Ralph Waldo Emerson (1803-82), is remembered for having observed: "All history is biography." I first heard this in a college class and have never forgotten it. When we stop to think about it we realize that history is, in fact, a vast storehouse of biographies, and the storehouse is ever growing. History is always with us, and we fail to study and learn from history at our peril. You may know the line from William Faulkner: "The past is never dead. It's not even past."

Of all times, our current situation reminds us how true it is: *The past is never dead. It's not even past.* As we study historical events and movements, in reality we are studying people. History *is* biography. When 2020 is studied by historians, they will study *people,* people such as Dr. Anthony Fauci and George Floyd.

On All Saints' Day we remember *people,* including some of the saints whose memory history preserves: people such as St. Francis of Assisi (1181-1226) and St. Teresa of Ávila (1515-82). But on All Saints' Day we also honor people whom *we* personally remember. In preparing this address I thought about my maternal grandmother, of whom history will take no notice. By the time I knew her she was a retired textile worker who had begun working in the mill before modern child labor laws went into effect. She had toiled in the mill her entire working life. All the time I knew her she was crippled from arthritis and walked with a cane, then a walker, and then was bedridden. She and her sister frequently kept my sister and me when we were young. One of the many things I remember about my grandmother is that whenever I would make a bad move while playing checkers she would slide the piece back to where it had started and say: "You didn't want to do that."

When I was a young boy there was nothing overtly religious

about me. I was just a kid. If the weather was warm, I would go out into grandma's yard and throw a baseball up in the air and catch it hundreds of times during the day. And when the weather was cool, I would throw a football up in the air and catch it hundreds of times a day. There was nothing unusually pious about me during my childhood. But my grandmother used to say that out of all her grandchildren: "Joey will be my preacher." How did she know?

When I went away to college I met a man named Robert Delp who taught American History, my favorite subject. Bob Delp was an ordained minister but had left the active pastorate for academia. I was a junior working for Dr. Delp as his student assistant when, in talking with me about my future, he volunteered: "You'll be an Episcopal priest someday." Twenty years old at that point, a junior in college, I literally laughed and said: "It would help if I were an Episcopalian." After all, how can a non-Episcopalian be an Episcopal priest? He let my laughter subside, looked me in the eye and said: "You'll be an Episcopal priest someday." How did he know before I knew?

I did not have a car in college. I could not afford one. There came a time when Bob Delp offered to take me to an Episcopal church one Sunday, and we went to Holy Comforter in our college town of Burlington, North Carolina. A couple of weeks later he said: "Let's go to a bigger Episcopal church." And the next Sunday we went to Holy Trinity in Greensboro. After that we went to Duke Chapel on a Sunday morning and worshiped in that magnificent Gothic structure built on the scale of the world's great cathedrals. All these years later I can still remember the preacher that day, José Míguez Bonino (1924-2012), of whom I had never heard. José Míguez Bonino, an Argentinian Methodist pastor and scholar, is one of the great ecumenical theologians of the twentieth century. I learned that day about José Míguez Bonino.

Something else happened that day. Looking up to the chapel's high ceiling, and around at all the beautiful windows and furnishings, and hearing a world-class theologian preaching, what clicked for me was: *There is a great big world 'out there.'* On that particular Sunday, in Duke Chapel, my world began to open up, and I have not looked back. History will take little notice of Dr. Robert Delp. He was a seldom-published classroom teacher in a small Southern college. But Bob Delp is a saint.

In the first parish I served there was a woman named Lillian Sherman. Lillian's husband had been Rector of St. Andrew's in Canton, North Carolina, years before my time there, and he had predeceased his wife by twenty years. Lillian, a native of Connecticut and still very much a New Englander in temperament, was quite active when I first went to St. Andrew's. When Lillian came to die, I can remember as vividly as if it were yesterday being with her in the ICU of St. Joseph's Hospital, Asheville. It was clear that she was dying, and when the moment presented itself I took her hand into mine and said: "Lillian, I will always pray for you." To which she replied: "And I, dear Joel, will always pray for you." At that precise moment the Communion of Saints started to make sense to me: the thought of Lillian Sherman, in eternity, praying for *me*. I have never forgotten that moment. History will not remember Lillian Sherman, but she is a saint.

I am telling you some of mine to invite you to think of yours. Who are those people who have shown you the way, who have inspired you? History may not remember them either, but they too are saints. Today is a day to *remember*, and to be grateful.

Just before our celebration of the Eucharist we will remember by name those beloved parishioners who have departed this life since last year's All Saints' observance. It is a poignant moment every year. And today, as we remember those beloved parishioners whom we love but see no longer, we also remember all former parishioners of St. Luke's on whose shoulders we stand. Everything we do is built on what they did, beginning in 1867, when St. Alban's Mission was begun in Cleveland, Tennessee. Today we remember and honor all those who have gone before us.

At noon today, as part of a national observance, our church bell will toll 230 times: one time for every thousand people who have died during this pandemic—*230,000 people*. We cannot allow ourselves to grow numb to these numbers, because the numbers represent *people*: people beloved of God, of their families, and of their friends.

It is important when we use a word to know what it means— what it really means. The word "saint" does not connote moral or ethical perfection. The *saints* are not people who were 'better' than the rest of us. The New Testament Greek word for "saints" means "set apart." That which is holy is set apart, and we are *all* set apart, marked as the beloved of God. Paul is quite clear that all of the baptized are saints (Romans 1:7; 1 Corinthians 1:2; 2 Corinthians 1:1; Philippians 1:1, 4:22; Ephesians 1:1). We are all set apart for God's service. There comes that moment in the baptismal liturgy when the celebrant anoints the baptized on the forehead and says: "...you are sealed by the Holy Spirit in Baptism and *marked* (emphasis mine) as Christ's own for ever."[1]

To honor the saints is not to place them on a pedestal they themselves would eschew. In honoring the saints, we are not honoring people who were inherently 'better' than we are. In commenting on this year's All Saints' Day observance, Angus Ritchie writes: "The earthly lives of the saints testify to an important spiritual reality. The closer human beings draw to God, the greater their awareness of their sinfulness is."[2] Sainthood has more to do with humility than superiority. Those closest to God are most aware of their humanity, and thus their dependence upon God's grace. Ritchie continues: "As they grow in virtue, the saints feel even more keenly both their imperfection, and their total dependence on the Lord."[3]

Matthew 5:1-12 is a portion of the greatest sermon ever preached, a sermon that preaches itself. Matthew 5:1-12 is comprised of what we call the Beatitudes. One of our great contemporary Bible scholars, Amy-Jill Levine, writes that the Beatitudes "...provide comfort and encourage action."[4] A great insight regarding the balanced messaging of the Beatitudes— they provide comfort *and* encourage action. There are moments when we need comfort, reassurance, and, in some cases, permission to 'come away for a while' and rest. In the thick of the pandemic, we need all three now as much as ever! But then there comes the time to act. Having been consoled and reassured, having rested, there comes the call to action. The Beatitudes both comfort us *and* push us forward.

The great reformer Martin Luther (1483-1546) observed that the work of Christ is both to console and to enliven. Here again we find a balance—consolation, reassurance—and then enlivenedness, renewal. The work of Christ is to console *and* to enliven. The Beatitudes embody the balanced message of Jesus —consolation and reassurance *and* the call to action. This is what the Beatitudes do—they both comfort us and urge us forward.

In John 10:10b we hear Jesus say: "I came that they may have life, and have it abundantly." *The New English Bible* translates: "I have come that men may have life, and may have it in all its fullness." The Beatitudes espouse fullness of life—life lived in and guided by the light of Christ.

In the middle of our passage we read: "Blessed are those who hunger and thirst for righteousness, for they will be filled. Blessed are the merciful, for they will receive mercy." The saints whom history remembers were not inherently better people than we are. They were not morally or ethically perfect. History remembers them for their concern for others. And their legacy is meant to be our inspiration.

In the Introduction to his classic book, *Voices of the Saints: A Year of Readings*, Bert Ghezzi writes: "We cannot misinterpret the message that all these saints declare: the joyful service of those in need."[5] Amen.

CHAPTER TWENTY-SIX

SYSTEMIC INJUSTICES ALL AROUND

8 November 2020 • Amos 5:18-24

¹⁸ Alas for you who desire the day of the LORD! Why do you want the day of the   LORD? It is darkness, not light; ¹⁹ as if someone fled from a lion, and was met by a bear; or went into the house and rested a hand against the wall, and was bitten by a snake. ²⁰ Is not the day of the LORD darkness, not light, and gloom with no brightness in it? ²¹ I hate, I despise your festivals, and I take no delight in your solemn assemblies. ²² Even though you offer me your burnt offerings and grain offerings, I will not accept them; and the offerings of well-being of your fatted animals I will not look upon. ²³ Take away from me the noise of your songs; I will not listen to the melody of your harps. ²⁴ But let justice roll down like waters, and   righteousness like an ever-flowing stream.

In Mark 6:1-4, we find an important historical kernel regarding the response to Jesus in the early days of his ministry. There we read about Jesus, in those early days, returning to his hometown of Nazareth and preaching in its synagogue. Mark records that while some in the crowd rejoice, others are less enthusiastic, and he tells us in 6:3 that some were asking: "'Is not this the carpenter, the son of Mary and brother of James and Joses and Judas and Simon, and are not his sisters here with us?' And they took offense at him." *Who does he think he is? We grew up with this guy.* In 6:4 Mark writes: "Then Jesus said to them, 'Prophets are not without honor, except in their hometown, and among their own kin, and in their own house.'" One of the more memorable insights of Jesus. Most prophets are accorded that status after they are dead, and most prophets' polling numbers are much higher after they have died than when they were alive and challenging people to reexamine their presuppositions and amend their ways.

We Episcopalians tend to love and cherish our worship traditions. Most of us like things done *decently and in order,* those words from Thomas Cranmer, Archbishop of Canterbury in the sixteenth century, who framed *The Book of Common Prayer.* Of course, *decently and in order* is not original to Cranmer. In 1 Corinthians 14:39-40 Paul writes: "So, my friends, be eager to prophesy, and do not forbid speaking in tongues; but all things should be done decently and in order." Worship services in our tradition tend to be carefully crafted, and then are carried out 'decently and in order' in accord with liturgical principles that can be traced all the way back to Paul.

We Episcopalians strongly identify with our Prayer Book tradition of structured liturgies offered decently and in order. And thus, hearing Amos 5:18-24 in the context of worship might jar us more than a little. Amos 5:21: "I hate, I despise your festivals, and I take no delight in your solemn assemblies." And in verse 23: "Take away from me the noise of your songs; I will not listen to the melody of your harps." I am certain that none of us climbed out of bed, got dressed, and came to church to have our venerable worship traditions challenged like this. That said, I have watched enough HGTV to know that oftentimes in real estate what matters most is *location, location, location*. And when it comes to interpreting Scripture, I submit to you that oftentimes what matters most is *context, context, context*.

In seeking to interpret Scripture faithfully and fruitfully, it is crucial that we have a sense of the historical context out of which the text arises. It is crucial as well to have a sense of the literary context in which the text resides. So what of this jarring passage from Amos, this challenge to solemn assemblies? We know that Amos wrote before the Assyrian conquest of 722 BC. Scholars consistently place Amos' writing some forty years earlier, ca. 760. In Amos' time, Assyria was not yet as powerful as it would become, and Egypt was uncustomarily weak in terms of its military strength. With Assyria still a developing power, and with Egypt weak, Israel was in the midst of a long season of prosperity. Times were good during Amos' lifespan, with Israel enjoying unchallenged peace and prosperity. While Amos' timeframe marks an era of wealth and prosperity for some, this was certainly not the case for all. In the Israel of Amos' day, the rich were getting richer while the poor were getting poorer. We know historically that land ownership, a matter of family or tribal prerogative in the past, by Amos' time was concentrated in a very small number of wealthy landowners. Again, *context, context, context*.

Amos' overarching concern is for social justice. On the one hand he sees wealth and prosperity among the privileged, while on the other hand he sees the poor being taken advantage of systemically. And so, with this historical context in mind, we can trust that Amos was not against worship in and of itself. What Amos *is* challenging is hypocrisy—'empty' worship— worship that is disconnected from the needs of the poor.

Amos is the earliest Old Testament prophet whose words we have recorded, but he is not the only prophet to be concerned about 'empty' religious language and observances (cf. Isaiah

1:10-17; Jeremiah 7:1-26; Hosea 6:6). But in this vein, in addition to Amos, perhaps the most memorable example is Micah 6:6-8. Micah 6:6-7 reads: "With what shall I come before the LORD, and bow myself before God on high? Shall I come before him with burnt offerings, with calves a year old? Will the LORD be pleased with thousands of rams, with ten thousands of rivers of oil? Shall I give my firstborn for my transgression, the fruit of my body for the sin of my soul?" Now here comes the part we like! Micah 6:8 is for many one of their favorite verses from the Old Testament: "He has told you, O mortal, what is good; and what does the LORD require of you but to do justice, and to love kindness, and to walk humbly with your God?" We do like that one! But it comes on the heels of two verses whose challenge mirrors that of Amos—scrutiny of religious traditions that have become disconnected from the needs of the poor and the marginalized. In considering the haunting instruction of Micah 6:8, Amos 5:24 also comes to mind: "But let justice roll down like waters, and righteousness like an ever-flowing stream." Here we encounter inspiring prophetic rhetoric whose teaching we readily affirm and yet find challenging to live up to. In literary context, both Amos 5:24 and Micah 6:8 follow on the heels of strong challenges to the status quo. Both verses remind us that worship always is to be concerned with, and connected to, the needs of the poor and the marginalized. Worship must not be allowed merely to speak to and affirm the prosperous. Worship also has to connect, *always*, with those who are suffering, those who are struggling, those on the margins who, along with the prosperous, are the beloved of God.

Amos lived in a time of peace and prosperity for many, and yet he also saw systemic injustices all around. It is as if Amos' message is something like this: God did not bring us out of slavery in Egypt so that we might become a nation of oppressors. *But let justice roll down like waters, and righteousness like an ever-flowing stream.*

In preparation for this address, I read in its entirety Dr. King's "I Have a Dream" speech given on August 28, 1963. Again, I read the speech in its entirety. *Context, context, context.* In reading the speech in its entirety, we are reminded just how brief the speech is. Brief yes, but carefully and artfully worded: laser focused and, in the end, irresistibly powerful. In the midst of the speech Dr. King puts forward an imagined rhetorical question from his critics: "When will you be satisfied?" And on that hot summer's day in 1963, Dr. King, a prophet for his and all future generations, answers to lasting effect in one of the seminal, transformative moments in American History: "We are not satisfied, and will not be satisfied until justice rolls down like water, and righteousness like a mighty stream."

Surely Amos understood the value of worship, as did Isaiah, Jeremiah, Hosea, and Micah. Amos must have understood the importance, indeed, the necessity, of forms of worship. But the Old Testament prophets and their descendants remind us that for worship to be authentic, efficacious, and offered with integrity, what we proclaim with our lips *must* show forth in our lives. In 1:22 the author of the Epistle of James, echoing the Hebrew prophets and, ultimately, Jesus himself, challenges all people of faith for all time: "But be doers of the word, and not merely hearers..." Amen.

CHAPTER TWENTY-SEVEN
A MIX OF PAIN AND HOPE

15 November 2020 • Psalm 90:1-8, 12

[1] Lord, you have been our refuge from one generation to another. [2] Before the mountains were brought forth, or the land and the earth were born, from age to age you are God. [3] You turn us back to the dust and say, "Go Back, O child of earth." [4] For a thousand years in your sight are like yesterday when it is past and like a watch in the night. [5] You sweep us away like a dream; we fade away suddenly like the grass. [6] In the morning it is green and flourishes; in the evening it is dried up and withered. [7] For we consume away in your displeasure; we are afraid because of your wrathful indignation. [8] Our iniquities you have set before you, and our secret sins in the light of your countenance. [12] So teach us to number our days that we may apply our hearts to wisdom.[1]

When in college I served as a Resident Assistant (RA) my junior and senior years. I was not an especially good RA; I only did it for the money. An RA was provided free room and board, and as an RA there was at least the prospect of a private room, which was deeply appealing to me, and along with the private room came a semi-private bathroom with shower. So, full disclosure, I was an RA strictly for the money and the prospect of having as little interaction with other people as possible! Suffice it to say, I was not from central casting.

In my early 20s, I could not have cared less about building community in the hall, one of an RA's primary duties. Nor did I care about being a member of the Residence Life team and working together with other people. We *can* change! Even saying these things gives me pause. Was I ever really that anti-social? The truth is, I was. It is also true to say that I have changed a lot over the years.

When it came time for Debbie and me to get married, I reached out to Dan, my last college roommate, and ended up speaking with his wife, Tammy. Tammy and I were on the RA staff together back in the day. In inviting Tammy and Dan to our wedding, after I gave the basic information about time and place, Tammy said: "Let me just make sure I've got this straight. Are you really a minister?" "Yes, I really am a minister." "And do you really have a church?" "Yes, I have a church." "And there are people in your church?" She was incredulous. So, when I mention periodically that I am a late bloomer, it is not just a line, and one of my passions in life is spotting and encouraging other late bloomers.

All of that is to say that as an RA I went to a workshop on time management at the beginning of my junior year. It was led by Jim Phillips, who called himself Captain Phillips, which I took to be a self-designation. Jim Phillips *was* our Director of

Safety and Security, and somehow it fell to him to offer the time management seminar for the RAs. I do not remember anything about the workshop save for the fact that, at the time, I thought it was worthwhile. I actually enjoyed it. The reason that workshop from my college days stands out in my mind all these years later is this: I am certain that it marked the first occasion when I really thought seriously about the importance and value of time.

Psalm 90 is about time. The Hebrew text indicates that it is a prayer of Moses, but most scholars regard this claim to be more an homage to Moses than a statement of fact. Most scholars think that Psalm 90 was actually written during the Babylonian Exile (ca. 598–538 BC.). Psalm 90 is about time in exile, time spent struggling, time in a situation of prolonged uncertainty. Psalm 90 has a lot to say to us today in 2020, in the midst of a global pandemic with no end in sight. There is that moment in Psalm 90:3 when the psalmist writes: "You turn us back to the dust and say, 'Go back, O child of earth.'" Here the psalmist is addressing the reality of death.

What the Israelites began to realize as the Babylonian Exile dragged on was that they were dying in a foreign country and did not know when God would lead them back to their beloved homeland. *You turn us back to the dust and say, 'Go back, O child of earth.'* With each passing day the exiled Jews experienced one more day away from home: one day closer to death in a foreign land.

Psalm 90 does turn encouraging as it goes on. By verses 13-17 the psalm is turning hopeful, even aspirational. Psalm 90 is in part a lament, and yet it ends on a hopeful, aspirational note, and the 'hinge,' the turning point, is verse 12: "So teach us to number our days that we may apply our hearts to wisdom." How does the psalmist envision bridging the gap between despair and hope? The answer lies in verse 12. In the end, Psalm 90 is about the importance and value of time.

Throughout the pandemic, and all that has come with it, I

keep being reminded of the correspondence between John Adams and Thomas Jefferson, our second and third presidents. In the time of their maturity, Adams wrote to Jefferson: "My friend, you and I have lived in serious times."[2] I cannot get that sentence out of my mind as the pandemic and all that has come with it grinds on. In the midst of the global pandemic, and in the midst of social stirring which brings with it a mix of pain and hope, 2020 is a year none of us will ever forget. Over the last several months, several people have said to me in one way or another: *We are watching history unfold right before our eyes.* It is true. We are experiencing the stuff of history in real time.

In the end, I think the psalmist was asking God: How long? How long are we going to be in exile? How long until we are free? To be sure, the particulars differ, and yet 2,500 years later we are asking the same questions, silently or aloud: How long? How long will we have to live with so much tension in our society? How long will we have to deal with so much uncertainty? How long will it be until we can get back to something that resembles normal?

"So teach us to number our days that we may apply our hearts to wisdom." In the end, the psalmist is asking: How long? What is it that you are trying to teach us? What is it that you would have us learn here in exile? So teach us *to number our days* that we may *apply our hearts to wisdom.* The NRSV translates verse 12: "So teach us to count our days that we may gain a wise heart."

Abraham Lincoln, arguably our greatest president, is remembered as having said: "I may walk slowly, but I never walk backward." In her commentary on Psalm 90, Nancy L. Declaissé-Walford writes: "The Israelites in exile in Babylon cannot return to the days of King David. They can only move forward."[3] The Jews in exile knew that they could not expect to return home to the glory days of King David, and yet they maintained hope. They trusted that God would deliver them. In due course they were freed, and exile was turned to exodus. In time, the Jews who returned to their homeland established a new normal. And generations later, a young Jewish woman who lived in a seemingly inconsequential agricultural village became pregnant, and gave birth to a baby boy, Jesus.

In 90:12, the psalmist asks for wisdom. One of the great scholars on the Psalter is Mitchell Dahood. In his commentary on Psalm 90, Dahood observes: "...the essence of Wisdom lies in recognizing the transience of human life."[4] Which means this: We cannot allow ourselves to spend too much time brooding over the past, nor can we allow ourselves to spend too much time being anxious about an uncertain future. The essence of wisdom, says Dahood, in the context of Psalm 90, is to live in the moment, to deal with the realities at hand and not allow the difficulties of the moment to negate an active hope for a brighter future. This spiritual wisdom from 2,500 years ago is particularly applicable in the moment that is now: "So teach *us* to number *our days* (emphasis mine) that we may apply our hearts to wisdom."

In reading Psalm 90, I am reminded of Psalm 118:24. I have found this verse deeply meaningful over the years, and it too has particular relevance in our time: "This is the day that the LORD has made; let us rejoice and be glad in it." Amen.

CHAPTER TWENTY-EIGHT
TRULY I TELL YOU

Christ the King Sunday
22 November 2020 • Matthew 25:31-46

[31] Jesus said, "When the Son of Man comes in his glory, and all the angels with him, then he will sit on the throne of his glory. [32] All the nations will be gathered before him, and he will separate people one from another as a shepherd separates the sheep from the goats, [33] and he will put the sheep at his right hand and the goats at the left. [34] Then the king will say to those at his right hand, 'Come, you that are blessed by my Father, inherit the kingdom prepared for you from the foundation of the world; [35] for I was hungry and you gave me food, I was thirsty and you gave me something to drink, I was a stranger and you welcomed me, [36] I was naked and you gave me clothing, I was sick and you took care of me, I was in prison and you visited me.' [37] Then the righteous will answer him, 'Lord, when was it that we saw you hungry and gave you food, or thirsty and gave you something to drink? [38] And when was it that we saw you a stranger and welcomed you, or naked and gave you clothing? [39] And when was it that we saw you sick or in prison and visited you?' [40] And

the king will answer them, 'Truly I tell you, just as you did it to one of the least of these who are members of my family, you did it to me.' [41] Then he will say to those at his left hand, 'You that are accursed, depart from me into the eternal fire prepared for the devil and his angels; [42] for I was hungry and you gave me no food, I was thirsty and you gave me nothing to drink, [43] I was a stranger and you did not welcome me, naked and you did not give me clothing, sick and in prison and you did not visit me.' [44] Then they also will answer, 'Lord, when was it that we saw you hungry or thirsty or a stranger or naked or sick or in prison, and did not take care of you?' [45] Then he will answer them, 'Truly I tell you, just as you did not do it to one of the least of these, you did not do it to me.' [46] And these will go away into eternal punishment, but the righteous into eternal life."

I graduated from Elon College in 1985. Elon College has evolved over the years into Elon University and is now a prestigious, fast-paced institution, truly on the cutting edge of higher education. But in my day, it was Elon College, and it was not particularly prestigious. We kept a slow pace and liked it that way. Back then, Elon offered a casual atmosphere and was, on the whole, a friendly campus. It did not take me long to learn the basic greeting at Elon College: "What's up?" That is what everyone said: "What's up?" And the typical response was: "Not much." That is a snapshot of Elon College in the early 1980s. Very casual, not prestigious—but a good place.

Given my less than spectacular high school transcript, I seriously doubt that I could get into Elon University as it now exists. But back in the day, Elon College was perfect for me—a late bloomer—just beginning to find my way. Back then, the faculty gave us a lot of personal attention, and a lot of affirmation when we excelled. Elon College set me on the path to a life that, before college, I never could have imagined for myself.

I have no idea what they do now, but, back in the day, there was a January term, "J-term," during which students took only one or two classes. It was the time to get in a class you needed to concentrate on if you expected to have a little trouble with it —like, say, Algebra! In January of 1982, I was a freshman at Elon and my dream of a college football career still had breath. I was an 'invited walk-on' with the football team, and we used J-Term for weight-training and conditioning. It was a great time to get a required core class in. The tradition for the football team was that, if you had not yet had it, one of the courses to take in J-term was Geology 101, aka "Rocks for Jocks." We really did call it that! And it was an interesting academic experience. The class was made up almost entirely of athletes, all needing to get in a core science class. Here is how it worked. At the end of each class session, we were given ten homework questions to work on. The next morning we could ask questions about all ten. So each day we divided up the questions among the group, deciding who would ask about which question. And, in fielding the questions, the professor would, in effect, answer them. We then proceeded to have a quiz each day, which bore a striking resemblance to the preceding day's homework. Geology 101: Rocks for Jocks.

Seemingly unrelated to all that, Christ the King Sunday is the last Sunday of the liturgical year, and the last Sunday before a new Advent. One of our great preachers in the Episcopal Church is Fleming Rutledge, and she has said in a sermon for Christ the King Sunday: "The Lord Jesus Christ is Lord and King over all creation! There is no other day of the Christian calendar quite like [it]. On [the] last Sunday of the liturgical year, we look both backward and forward."[1] On Christ the King Sunday we look forward to Advent and backward on the liturgical year that is reaching its conclusion. A way to frame Christ the King Sunday is to say that it puts an exclamation point on the liturgical year. Everything we are meant to have learned and affirmed

in Advent, Christmas, Epiphany, Lent, Easter and Pentecost—
everything that we are meant to have learned and affirmed over
a year's worth of worship—is summed up in the statement: *The
Lord Jesus Christ is Lord and King over all creation*. Even in 2020.

Fleming Rutledge is right. In celebrating Christ the King, we
look both backward and forward. On Christ the King Sunday we
wrap up a full liturgical year and are on the cusp of a new season
of Advent. The wreath and the candles are pre-positioned in the
sacristy as we speak. They will appear next week.

On Wednesday mornings a small but dedicated group of us
are enjoying a weekly online Bible study led by N.T. Wright. In
our conversation this past week, we talked about the Benedictine motto: "Always we begin again." It is a Benedictine mantra.
There is a wonderful devotional book by that title, *Always We
Begin Again: The Benedictine Way of Living*, by John McQuiston II. I
recommend the book highly. Advent marks a new beginning
each year, a new liturgical cycle. I suspect that Advent 2020 will
be even more meaningful than ever as we begin a new, a fresh, a
hopeful liturgical year. *Always we begin again* may hold more
promise now than ever.

Matthew 25:31-46 offers a picture of Jesus' teaching on the
last judgment. When I left Elon College and went on to graduate
studies at Candler School of Theology, Emory University, one of
the faculty members was Fred Craddock, in his heyday as one of
the great preachers of the time. Dr. Craddock was at the top of
his game in the mid-1980s. He says in a sermon for Christ the
King Sunday: "The Bible conveys the unwavering conviction that
history and human life have direction and purpose. Life and
history are not according to chance or caprice or accident."[2] He
continues: "History has an Alpha and an Omega, a beginning
and an end."[3] And thus, *always we begin again*, until we cannot.

Fred Craddock continues in that Christ the King Sunday
sermon (and here is where Geology 101 comes back in): "If we
know we are going to face a final exam of one question *and we*

are told by the examiner what that question is to be (emphasis minc),
is it not reasonable to suppose that one question would gather
to itself the interest and the energies and the concerns of all of
us?"[4] And thus, the allusion to Geology 101. Craddock frames
the last judgment in terms of one question. Imagine, he
suggests, taking an exam consisting of one question, and you
can know *the* question in advance. So what is it that Craddock is
suggesting is *the* question? What is the one question we will
face at the final judgment? Craddock's suggestion, based on
Matthew 25:31-46, is this: *How did you respond to human need?*

Back to Fleming Rutledge, who says regarding 25:31-46:
"The originality of Matthew's Gospel is its unique stress on two
things at once: the cosmic divinity of Jesus, and at the same
time, his identification with the lowest and least among human
beings."[5] What a wonderful summation of Matthew's message
in 25:31-46. Jesus is Christ the King, and at the same time he
cares for the humble, the poor, those on the margins.

Carol Harrison, Lady Margaret Professor of Divinity, University of Oxford, writes in a sermon for Christ the King Sunday
that while Christ is 'King,' he is also "shepherd, door, lamb,
light, bread."[6] Christ is King. But he is also humble, accessible,
deeply caring—especially for those on the margins of society.
Matthew 25:35-36: "For I was hungry and you gave me food, I
was thirsty and you gave me something to drink, I was a
stranger and you welcomed me, I was naked and you gave me
clothing, I was sick and you took care of me, I was in prison and
you visited me." And then Matthew 25:40: "And the king will
answer them: 'Truly I tell you, just as you did it to one of the
least of these who are members of my family, you did it to me.'"
In Matthew's picture of the final judgment, Jesus is portrayed as
framing our final examination in terms of one all-encompassing,
all-important question: How did you respond to human need?

One of my favorite authors is Sam Keen. Years ago in reading
Keen's book, *Hymns to an Unknown God: Awakening the Spirit in*

Everyday Life, I came across a particular passage that has stuck with me ever since. It occurs to me that the passage provides a fitting way to end this reflection on Matthew 25:31-46. It is a fitting way to frame that one all-encompassing, all-important question on our *final exam:*

> In the spiritual journey, the compass unfailingly points toward compassion. This spiritual compass is the equivalent of the satellite Ground Position System... Inscribe this single word on your heart—"compassion." Whenever you are confused, keep heading in the direction that leads toward deepening your love and care for all living beings, including yourself, and you will never stray far from the path to fulfillment.[7]

Amen.

CHAPTER TWENTY-NINE

ATTENTION

First Sunday of Advent
29 November 2020 • Mark 13:24-37

[24] Jesus said, "But in those days, after that suffering, the sun will be darkened, and the moon will not give its light, [25] and the stars will be falling from heaven, and the powers in the heavens will be shaken. [26] Then they will see 'the Son of Man coming in clouds' with great power and glory. [27] Then he will send out the angels, and gather his elect from the four winds, from the ends of the earth to the ends of heaven. [28] "From the fig tree learn its lesson: as soon as its branch becomes tender and puts forth its leaves, you know that summer is near. [29] So also, when you see these things taking place, you know that he is near, at the very gates. [30] Truly I tell you, this generation will not pass away until all these things have taken place. [31] Heaven and earth will pass away, but my words will not pass away. [32] "But about that day or hour no one knows, neither the angels in heaven, nor the Son, but only the Father. [33] Beware, keep alert; for you do not know when the time will come. [34] It is like a man going on a journey, when he leaves home and puts his slaves in charge,

each with his work, and commands the doorkeeper to be on the watch. [35] Therefore, keep awake—for you do not know when the master of the house will come, in the evening, or at midnight, or at cockcrow, or at dawn, [36] or else he may find you asleep when he comes suddenly. [37] And what I say to you I say to all: Keep awake."

W hile watching the news this past Friday, I saw a disturbing scene which was captured on video. People were crowded together in great numbers before dawn. There was pushing and shoving and shouting; expletives had to be bleeped out. The tension and anger were palpable, and some of the people in the video were very nearly coming to blows. In the midst of a pandemic, why would there be such a crowd in the predawn hours? Of course, to shop for Christmas. They were Christmas shopping!

On the same day I saw a very different scene. I was going home from the YMCA after sunset, and while driving I realized how many people had put up their Christmas lights over the Thanksgiving holiday. Making my way home in the darkness, it was good to see light.

The First Sunday of Advent marks the beginning of a new liturgical year, a new liturgical cycle. "Always we begin again" say the Benedictines. *Always* we begin again.

One way to frame Advent is with the juxtaposition of the words *already* and *not yet*. During Advent we prepare to commemorate the first coming of Christ, the Incarnation. The first Sunday of Advent marks the beginning, in a liturgical context, of our preparation for Christmas. The Episcopal Church is at its best liturgically and theologically as we prepare for and then celebrate Christmas. But Advent has a second focus which does not get nearly as much attention. Advent is also a time to remember the promised second coming of Christ, the promise that history is inexorably moving forward to its fulfillment when God's kingdom will come in its fullness. So beginning today, we look *back* to that first Christmas, and we look *forward* to the second coming of Christ. Advent—the season of *already* and *not yet*.

Just a couple of months ago I heard a quotation that has shaped my life ever since. One of the great actors of all time, Laurence Olivier, was asked: What is the key to a great performance? How do you deliver a great performance? Olivier replied: "It takes two things: the humility to prepare, and the confidence to pull it off." What a great combination. A great performance takes the humility to prepare, every time. And after that preparation has been made, a great performance requires confidence. What a great recipe regarding how to be at our best: humility *and* confidence.

The great tennis player and shaper of American social life, Arthur Ashe, once observed that the key to confidence is preparation. When we are prepared, when we have put in the work, then we can be confident. The word "confidence" does not in any way carry with it an inherent connotation of arrogance. Confidence is *con-fidence*: "with faith," or, "with trust." To be confident in life, to have faith, to trust in ourselves, depends on preparation. We prepare, we put in the work, and *then* we can be con-fident.

When I am out driving, I love to read church signs, rear window stickers and bumper stickers. I saw two that caught my eye just this week. As a minivan pulled past and then eased in front of me, I saw its rear window sticker that said: "You just got passed by a minivan." The other rear window sticker that I noticed this week was just about a block and a half south of here, right in front of the shop that sells athletic wear. That one said: "The more I prepare, the luckier I am." You can get a lot of truth in a rear window sticker. *The more I prepare, the luckier I am.*

Advent is meant to be a time of preparation, making ready

for a joyful celebration of Christmas. At the same time, Advent is a reminder that history is moving forward to its fulfillment. Again, a way to frame Advent is *already* and *not yet.*

To keep a proper Advent is, in many ways, counter-cultural in our society. I was in a local business several weeks ago and realized that the music being piped in was Elvis' "Here Comes Santa Claus." It was 70 degrees outside in mid-November! That said, the cultural trappings of 'the Holidays' are what they are. The proverbial 'snowball' is rolling down the hill, and at one level resistance is futile. Culture will observe this season as it chooses, and we can do very little about that. Nonetheless, we still have a choice to make now that Advent is upon us. We can choose to mark this season as holy, as potentially transformative in our spiritual lives. Whatever the inevitable cultural trappings, we still get to choose: Will I keep a holy, meaningful season of Advent?

One of the great preachers of the Episcopal Church is Fleming Rutledge. Fleming Rutledge has spoken and written a lot over the years about Advent, and there is a collection of her work titled A*dvent: The Once and Future Coming of Jesus Christ.* Please just linger over that subtitle for a moment—*The Once and Future Coming of Jesus Christ.* Already *and* not yet.

There are three brief quotations that I would like to share with you from Fleming Rutledge's book on Advent. The first: "The church calendar is not the same as the world's calendar."[1] The *choice* to keep a meaningful Advent season is before us. The second quotation: Advent is meant to be "the deepest place in the church year."[2] This is a strong statement. Consider how much there is to ponder in Advent, how much there is to meditate on, to reflect on, to pray about. We can get caught up in the rush, the cultural trappings of the season, or we can dive deep into the *deepest* place in the church year—Advent. And the third quotation: "Watchfulness and readiness are the hallmarks of the Advent life."[3] We may think, with the realization that 'the season' is upon us, primarily in terms of busyness, even in the midst of the pandemic. Or, in 2020, we may get caught up in thinking how different *this* season will be. A perfectly valid realization. And yet, when we consider what Advent is meant to be, what Advent is meant to mean to us, Fleming Rutledge reminds us: *Watchfulness* and *readiness* are the hallmarks of the Advent life.

Jesus says in Mark 13:33: "Beware, keep alert; for you do not know when the time will come." And then in verses 35-36: "keep awake — for you do not know when the master of the house will come...or else he may find you asleep when he comes suddenly." And then in verse 37: "And what I say to you I say to all: Keep awake." Here Jesus is teaching, prophesying, that history will reach its fulfillment. There will come a time when humanity knows God's kingdom in its fullness. In the meantime our attitude is to be one of wakefulness, preparedness: present to each moment, not weighed down by worry over the past nor paralyzed by anxiety regarding the future. As followers of Christ, we are to be awake, watchful, ready. *Watchfulness* and *readiness* are the hallmarks of the Advent life.

The English priest and spiritual writer Michael Mayne gave an Advent sermon in St. Thomas Parish, Salisbury, in 1998, which included these words: "Many people think that the Christian faith is basically saying 'Do this!' or 'Don't do that!' It isn't. It's saying: 'Look! Pay attention! Look at God and his creation and each other with changed eyes because of what you see in Christ.'"[4] On that Advent Sunday nearly two decades ago, Mayne urged his hearers: Do not think of the Christian faith so much as a list of rules. Do not be so quick to frame Christianity in terms of a list of dos and don'ts. Rather, see Christianity as promoting an attitude of awareness. Pay attention to the moment. Be aware of all that is happening. And then, in that memorable phrasing: Look at God and his creation and each other with *changed eyes* because of what you see in Christ. This is the *already* component of Advent. How we see in the present is meant to be changed, transformed because of what happened *already* in that first Christmas. See the world with *changed eyes* because of what you see in Christ. The author of the Gospel of John puts it this way in 1:14: "And the Word became flesh and lived among us, and we have seen his glory..." Already.

There is a story of a great spiritual teacher who was at the point of death, with his students gathered around him in the hope of receiving one last bit of wisdom from him. The students were gathered at the bedside of their dying teacher and their spokesperson (think of Simon Peter) said: "Teacher, we are here. Have you anything to say to us?" The teacher gathered all of his strength and said: "Attention." The students leaned in. Everyone inched a little closer. Again the spokesperson for the group said: "We are here, Teacher. What is it that you would have us hear?" And again the teacher summoned all the strength he had left and said: "Attention." The students inched in even a little closer, and just one more time their spokesperson said: "Teacher, we are here. What would you have us learn?" And this time the teacher really did summon the last ounce of energy and strength he had and he said: "*ATTENTION!*" The students finally got it. That *is* the teaching. Attention. Amen.

CHAPTER THIRTY

IN MEMORY OF TYLER HERNDON

Third Sunday of Advent
13 December 2020 • 1 Thessalonians 5:16-24

[16] Rejoice always, [17] pray without ceasing, [18] give thanks in all circumstances; for this is the will of God in Christ Jesus for you. [19] Do not quench the Spirit. [20] Do not despise the words of prophets, [21] but test everything; hold fast to what is good; [22] abstain from every form of evil. [23] May the God of peace himself sanctify you entirely; and may your spirit and soul and body be kept sound and blameless at the coming of our Lord Jesus Christ. [24] The one who calls you is faithful, and he will do this.

The words we use matter and should be chosen carefully. Of course, at certain times the stakes are higher than at other times. Some occasions call for more careful speech, more precise, measured wording, than other occasions. But, in the end, our words always matter.

In our culture, we are increasingly dealing with the imprecise use of words. Social media has a lot to do with this. So many people now have such easy access to technology that allows us to say anything we want, whenever we want, whether we have thought it through or not. We have all become familiar with the phrasing: "I just wanted to get it out there." Well, not everything needs to be gotten out there. The legendary college basketball coach Dean Smith used to say: "I say what's on my mind. I just don't say everything that's on my mind." There is another, rather new entry into our lexicon that we hear with increasing frequency: "He/She (whether a politician, athlete, or some other celebrity) has had to walk that back." Unfortunately, we hear it all the time now: *He's had to walk it back*. Which is another way of saying that what was said is not true, or at least not fully accurate.

Increasingly, we find ourselves dealing with the imprecise use of words. That said, I am sure that Paul has chosen his words carefully and employs them with precision: "Rejoice always, pray without ceasing, give thanks in all circumstances..." These words have a flow, and a spiritual ring to them. They constitute strong biblical rhetoric. And yet, when fully taken to heart, do they ring true? Particularly in a moment such as ours, with so many challenges before us all at once. Can we really rejoice *always*? Can we really be expected *always* to remember to be prayerful?

1 Thessalonians is the oldest book in the New Testament. Of course, the Gospels refer to earlier history, but in terms of a book in its final, written form, 1 Thessalonians is the oldest book in the New Testament. In it, Paul is writing to a young church that has experienced a tumultuous split from its synagogue of origin. We can read about that in Acts 17:1-10. In Acts, Luke references the birth of the church in Thessalonica and the pain that was caused when that subset of the Jewish synagogue left to form a Christian congregation. We can be sure that in 1 Thessalonians Paul writes with intention and chooses his words carefully. He knows that there are hurt feelings. He knows all too well the reality of tension in the local

faith community. With purpose, into a specific context in which the stakes are high, Paul encourages the congregation: Rejoice *always*. Pray *without ceasing*. Give thanks *in all circumstances*.

No doubt Paul's words are carefully chosen. We know this in part because he offers them again later in the Letter to the Philippians. In Philippians 4:4 we read: "Rejoice in the Lord always; again I will say, Rejoice." What we hear in 1 Thessalonians, Paul says twice in one sentence in Philippians. His words are thoughtfully, intentionally, and precisely chosen. It is important to remember about Philippians that it is one of the 'prison letters.' Paul wrote Philippians from jail! While imprisoned for his faith, Paul can still say with clear intention: *Rejoice in the Lord always*. Not, Rejoice at *everything* happening. But, Rejoice *in the Lord* always.

In the ancient world, it was labor intensive to write a letter. Paul could not just shoot an e-mail to Thessalonica. The writing and delivery of a letter in the ancient world took far more effort than it does for us; and thus, people in the ancient world chose their words carefully, and with precision. Paul means what he says in both 1 Thessalonians and Philippians: Rejoice in the Lord, maintain an attitude of prayerfulness, and give thanks to God—always.

Today, we hear Paul's words in the midst of a global pandemic of which we are all increasingly fatigued. Also, we hear his words in the midst of continuing social unrest. Thus, in our historical context, these words are jarring. They certainly are challenging. Even now, are we to *rejoice*? Can we really give thanks in *all* circumstances? Paul would say yes, knowing full well the challenges of life. Paul lived as full a life as a person in the ancient world could live. He was highly educated, well-traveled, of Jewish background and training, while also a Roman citizen. In mid-life, he experienced the risen Christ and went from being a zealous persecutor of Christians to the first great

Christian missionary. Even from jail, Paul's faith is such that he can say to Christians: *Rejoice in the Lord, always, and be thankful.*

Paul had no use for empty religious rhetoric. And 2,000 years later, neither do I. On Friday evening, I was half-watching the national news while multi-tasking. At one point I saw the words "Mt. Holly, North Carolina" in the 'crawl' on the bottom of the screen, which never happens. Mt. Holly is my hometown. My parents still live there. My hometown made the national news because a 25-year-old police officer was shot and killed Friday night while responding to a burglary. His name is Tyler Herndon. Today is his birthday. *Today* he would have been 26 years old. As you might imagine, this shocking and tragic story has been on my mind all weekend. Where Tyler Herndon was shot is less than a mile from where my parents live, where Debbie and I will be a week-and-a-half from now when we go to celebrate Christmas with my folks. I say all of that to say this: When Paul wrote the words recorded in 1 Thessalonians 5:16-24, he meant them. And my words in this moment—I mean them. Whatever life gives us, in the end, we are meant to find it within us to know, and to remember, that we are loved by Love. And for Love's presence we can always, in the end, be grateful, come what may.

It is important for us to remember that joy and happiness are not precise synonyms. Happiness tends to be dependent on external circumstances. Things are either going well for us or not. We are either having a good day or not. We either feel good or not. Happiness comes and goes. One moment we may be happy, and the next moment not, depending on circumstances. But joy is meant to be found in a deeper place. Joy is qualitatively 'other.' Joy is more than happiness. It is God's grace. Paul encourages both his original audience and us: Remember, you are loved by Love. And for that we are meant to be joyful, and thankful.

It is important to know that in the Greek of the New Testament "joy" and "grace" come from the same Greek stem. They have the same root derivation—joy *and* grace. We think about grace as a gift. Well, joy comes from the same Greek stem. Joy is God's love, ever present within us, including when we need it the most.

Right now, we need it. We need healing—physically, spiritually, and culturally. We need an end to this pandemic. And somehow, through the grace of God and through the good intentions of God's people, we in this country have to learn how to embrace each other and live together in peace. We have never needed Love more than now. And now, more than any other time in recent memory, culture needs the Church to meet the moment, to set an example of what it means to love one another, to forgive one another, and to work—really work—for healing and reconciliation.

Paul chooses his words carefully in 1 Thessalonians: "Rejoice always, pray without ceasing, give thanks in all circumstances; for this is the will of God in Christ Jesus for you." Amen.

CHAPTER THIRTY-ONE

IT MAKES A DIFFERENCE
WHAT YOU BELIEVE

First Sunday after Christmas
27 December 2020 • John 1:1-18

[1] In the beginning was the Word, and the Word was with God, and the Word was God. [2] He was in the beginning with God. [3] All things came into being through him, and without him not one thing came into being. What has come into being [4] in him was life, and the life was the light of all people. [5] The light shines in the darkness, and the darkness did not overcome it. [6] There was a man sent from God, whose name was John. [7] He came as a witness to testify to the light, so that all might believe through him. [8] He himself was not the light, but he came to testify to the light. [9] The true light, which enlightens everyone, was coming into the world. [10] He was in the world, and the world came into being through him; yet the world did not know him. [11] He came to what was his own, and his own people did not accept him. [12] But to all who received him, who believed in his name, he gave power to become children of God, [13] who were born, not of blood or of the will of the flesh or of the will

of man, but of God. [14] And the Word became flesh and lived among us, and we have seen his glory, the glory as of a father's only son, full of grace and truth. [15] (John testified to him and cried out, "This was he of whom I said, 'He who comes after me ranks ahead of me because he was before me.'") [16] From his fullness we have all received, grace upon grace. [17] The law indeed was given through Moses; grace and truth came through Jesus Christ. [18] No one has ever seen God. It is God the only Son, who is close to the Father's heart, who has made him known.

In his commentary on John 1:1-18, commonly referred to as the Prologue, Fred Craddock states: "...it makes a difference what you believe."[1] At one level that sounds like stating the obvious. And at one level it is. *It makes a difference what you believe.* And yet, taken at a deeper level, the statement is a profoundly important reminder and, in the end, is lastingly instructive.

If we want infancy narratives regarding the birth of Jesus we go to Matthew and Luke. In introducing his Gospel, John chooses a different approach. What we get from John is one of the great discrete passages in all the Bible. In John 1:1-2 we read: "In the beginning was the Word, and the Word was with God, and the Word was God. He was in the beginning with God." One of our great contemporary preachers is Barbara Brown Taylor, "BBT" as she is known by many. She notes regarding our passage that in framing his Gospel, John chooses to tell "a cosmic story...a second Genesis..."[2] The primary definition of "cosmic" refers to "extra-terrestrial vastness, the universe vis-à-vis the earth alone."[3] The secondary definition of cosmic is: "characterized by greatness especially in extent, intensity, or comprehensiveness."[4] In both senses of the word, John begins his Gospel with a *cosmic* story. N.T. Wright notes in his commentary on the Prologue: "...it isn't just about the birth of

Jesus, but about the full meaning of everything he was, and is, and did."[5]

My father was a truck driver for much of his career. He drove a truck for decades, including during my formative years. He tells the story of working on the warehouse dock as a very young man when his supervisor came over one day and said: "I need you to take a truck to Columbus, Georgia." My father replied: "But I'm not a driver." To which his supervisor said: "You will be when you get back." And that is how my father became a truck driver—in one day! He simply was told that he was one.

So all the time I was growing up, at the end of each workday my father would 'call in' at around 4:00 pm. He left very early in the mornings, did his run, drove back home, and at 4:00 pm he would call in to get his assignment for the next day. If he was not familiar with that site he would get out his map, and I would look at it with him and watch as he plotted how he would get to his next day's destination. I can remember those moments to this day. So, as much as I appreciate GPS and Google Earth and all other new technologies, I still carry a road atlas in my car—always. In all my travels, I am never without it. I love looking at maps so much that right now, in the nightstand closest to where I sleep there is a road atlas in the drawer! That is how much I appreciate maps and what they can tell us.

What John chooses to do in 1:1-18 is to give us a road map of his entire Gospel narrative. The Prologue to John tells us exactly where his Gospel is headed. And in 1:14 we get a preview of its overarching meaning: "And the Word became flesh and lived among us, and we have seen his glory, the glory as of a father's only son, full of grace and truth." The essential message of the Gospel is crystallized in one verse: *And the Word became flesh and lived among us...*

Fred Craddock, a mentor to Barbara Brown Taylor, says of the Prologue: "All the qualities one could ask of a text are here:

truth that is timeless, ideas which stretch mind and imagination, affirmations that are lifegiving, significance for every human being, and a central theme which gives the passage unity and completeness of thought."[6] The Prologue represents John's literary artistry at its finest, and in it John points to the central theme that gives everything else in the Gospel its unity and completeness: *And the Word became flesh and lived among us, and we have seen his glory, the glory as of a father's only son, full of grace and truth.* Craddock goes on to say that this text "resists...mastery, towering above all the homilies which have attempted to reveal its heights."[7] No preacher can possibly fully encapsulate in one sermon the theological richness of the Prologue, and each time we hear the Prologue to John we are reminded of its majesty and, ultimately, of its singular standing in the Gospel tradition. Craddock observes further in his introductory comments on the Prologue that it is "hardly surpassed when expressing the *inexpressible* (emphasis mine)."[8] When we try our best to convey what we believe about God in Christ we come up short to what John has accomplished in 1:1-18.

It makes a difference what you believe. Last Sunday morning on British television, Justin Welby, Archbishop of Canterbury, said in an interview: "Christmas isn't cancelled. Adjustments will have to be made to our celebrations. Plans and traditions will have to be altered, but Christmas isn't cancelled." *The light shines in the darkness, and the darkness did not overcome it.*

On Christmas morning 2020, the last thing that we in this region needed was an explosion in downtown Nashville at the AT&T facility. But that is exactly what happened. Upon learning of the incident, my thoughts went immediately to all of our loved ones in Nashville. There are so many connections between households here in our community and there in Nashville. We know now that as soon as the alert went out regarding the threat of the bombing, police officers and other first responders courageously and selflessly rushed to the scene immediately and began working to evacuate people. We will never know for sure just how many lives were saved because of their heroic actions. *The light shines in the darkness, and the darkness did not overcome it.*

More from Fred Craddock regarding the Prologue: "Of course, the writer is realistic enough to know there is evil, darkness, and death in the world, but these are due to human choice and not to anything in the nature of the world."[9] In coming to grips with the bombing in Nashville on, of all days, Christmas Day, I could not help but think about the pandemic that we have all been dealing with for so long now, about all of the nurses and doctors and first responders and cleaning crews who have been serving so courageously and selflessly for months now. I thought about teachers in our area who have served selflessly and faithfully during this difficult time. We all owe so much to those who, at great risk to themselves, serve the public good and follow their vocation of service even now in these difficult, trying, and exhausting days. As we honor people who are on the front lines, we are reminded that following the best safety protocols and the best medical practices has nothing to do with either of the colors red or blue. It is simply a *human* choice, a *spiritual* choice, to follow the best medical guidance and safety protocols that science can offer. This is what all of us can do to show our belief in the dignity and value of all human life. During the pandemic, there are so many people who are living and serving courageously and selflessly. The darkness is not overcoming the goodness in humanity.

Scholars think that the Gospel of John is the latest of the four canonical Gospels, probably written ca. 90-100 AD, some sixty years after Easter. Given this scenario, John is thus written from a different perspective, and with more hindsight, than Matthew, Mark, or Luke. One way to note the differences between John and the Synoptics is to refer to 'Johannine distinctives.' Up until the Passion, the Gospel of John has a different sequence of events, a different cast of characters—a different texture—than Matthew, Mark, or Luke. One of the biggest differences is the Prologue. John makes clear that he is indeed telling a cosmic story. In reading the Prologue we cannot help being reminded of Genesis: "In the *beginning* (emphasis mine) was the Word, and the Word was with God, and the Word was God."

We have the Prologue as our text for this First Sunday after Christmas. John's Gospel also contains an epilogue. Chapter 21 gives every appearance of being an epilogue, and thus it is likely that the original version of John ended at 20:30-31: "Now Jesus did many other signs in the presence of his disciples, which are not written in this book. But these are written so that you may come to believe that Jesus is the Messiah, the Son of God, and that through believing you may have life in his name."

It makes a difference what you believe. Amen.

ACKNOWLEDGMENTS

My thanks to all who heard the original offerings of the contents of this book during the unforgettable year of 2020, and for your encouraging comments—both in-person and online.

Thanks to Andrea Spraggins for her dedication and diligence in typing the original drafts of these addresses for the parish archive, and for all other invaluable assistance with technology. Thanks to Isaac Doty, who has developed and facilitated the online offerings of St. Luke's from the beginning of the pandemic to now. Isaac you are forever the architect of our exceptional online platforms.

Thanks to Carl Holladay, Brian Cole, Brenda Orcutt, Mark Chapman, Mark Oakley, and Jeff Ringer for your gracious support of this book, and for our friendship. Thanks to John R. Mabry of Apocryphile Press for your interest in and support of this project.

Thanks to my mother, Pansy Huffstetler, for instilling in me a love of Scripture and the recognition of its primacy. Thanks to Alison Mayne for your encouragement and support for more than a decade, and for our friendship. In tending Michael's voice I found my own.

Thanks to Patricia Pierce, who graciously suggested the undertaking of this project, not knowing that it was secretly under way(!) and for going so far as to suggest the title, *Changed Eyes*.

Thanks to our dear friends, Marilyn and Al Hoke. Much of the initial work on this book took place at the kitchen table at

Alys. We will never be able to express fully what your friendship means to us.

Finally, thank you to my wife, Debbie, who has partnered with me at every stage of this project, including offering invaluable editorial assistance and typing numerous versions of the 'final' draft. Thank you, my love, for your support of and help with this book, and for all else. And now, on to the next chapter of OUR ADVENTURE.

NOTES

1. HER ACHIEVEMENT IS REMARKABLE

1. Fred B. Craddock, *The Cherry Log Sermons* (Louisville, KY: Westminster John Knox Press, 2001), 49.
2. *Ibid.*
3. *Ibid.*
4. Gail R. O'Day, "Gospel of John." *Women's Bible Commentary*. Third Edition. Carol A. Newsom, Sharon H. Ringe and Jacqueline E. Lapsley, Editors (Louisville, KY: Westminster John Knox Press, 2012), 521.
5. *Ibid.*
6. *Ibid.*
7. Susan E. Hylen, *Imperfect Believers: Ambiguous Characters in the Gospel of John* (Louisville, KY: Westminster John Knox Press, 2009), 42.
8. Robert Kysar, *John: The Maverick Gospel*. Revised Edition (Louisville, KY: Westminster John Knox Press, 1993), 151.

2. OUT OF THE DARK, AND INTO THE LIGHT

1. N. T. Wright, *John for Everyone: Part One, Chapters 1-10*. Second Edition (Louisville, KY: Westminster John Knox Press, 2004), 139.

3. CHANGED EYES

1. N. T. Wright, *John for Everyone: Part One, Chapters 1-10*. Second Edition (Louisville, KY: Westminster John Knox Press, 2004), 139.
2. Gail R. O'Day and Susan E. Hylen, *John*. Westminster Bible Companion. Patrick D. Miller and David L. Bartlett, Series Editors (Louisville, KY: Westminster John Knox Press, 2006), 101.
3. Frances Taylor Gench, *Encounters with Jesus: Studies in the Gospel of John* (Louisville, KY: Westminster John Knox Press, 2007), 74.
4. *Ibid.*, 75.

4. A SERVANT'S HEART

1. *The HarperCollins Study Bible*. Wayne A. Meeks, General Editor (New York: HarperCollins, Publishers, Inc., 1993), 1895.
2. Leon Morris, *The Gospel According to Matthew*. The Pillar New Testament Commentary. D. A. Carson, General Editor (Grand Rapids, MI: William B. Eerdmans Publishing Company, 1992), 523.
3. Craig L. Blomberg, *Matthew*. The New American Commentary, Vol. 22. David S. Dockery, General Editor (Nashville, TN: B&H Publishing Group, 1992), 312.
4. Joe Kapolyo, "Matthew." *African Bible Commentary*. Tokunboh Adeyemo, General Editor (Grand Rapids, MI: Zondervan, 2006), 1180.
5. Donald A. Hagner, *Matthew 14-28*. Word Biblical Commentary, Vol. 33B. Bruce M. Metzger, David A. Hubbard and Glenn W. Barker, General Editors (Nashville, TN: Thomas Nelson Publishers, 1995), 597.

5. THE BONDS OF CHRISTIAN COMMUNITY

1. Fleming Rutledge, *The Undoing of Death: Sermons for Holy Week and Easter* (Grand Rapids, MI: William B. Eerdmans Publishing Company, 2002), 79.
2. *Ibid.*

6. THE VITAL IMPORTANCE OF CHRISTIAN COMMUNITY

1. Michael Mayne, *Dust that Dreams of Glory: Reflections on Lent and Holy Week*. Joel W. Huffstetler, Editor (London: Canterbury Press, 2017), 29.
2. Fleming Rutledge, *The Undoing of Death: Sermons for Holy Week and Easter* (Grand Rapids, MI: William B. Eerdmans Publishing Company, 2002), 74.

7. HAVING NEW EYES

1. Samuel T. Lloyd III, *Sermons from the National Cathedral: Soundings for the Journey* (New York: Rowman & Littlefield Publications, Inc., 2013), 307.
2. "Marcel Proust Quotes." https://www.brainyquote.com/quotes/marcel_proust_107111.

9. WHAT MATTERS MOST

1. *Webster's Ninth New Collegiate Dictionary* (Springfield, MA: Merrriam-Webster Inc., Publishers, 1987), 571.
2. Frederick Buechner, *Secrets in the Dark: A Life in Sermons* (New York: Harper-SanFrancisco, 2006), 256.
3. *Ibid.*
4. David P. Moessner, "Reading Luke's Gospel as Ancient Hellenistic Narrative: Luke's Narrative Plan of Israel's Suffering Messiah as God's Saving 'Plan' for the World." *Reading Luke: Interpretation, Reflection, Formation.* Scripture and Hermeneutics Series, Vol. 6. Craig G. Bartholomew, Joel B. Green and Anthony C. Thiselton, Editors (Grand Rapids, MI: Zondervan, 2005), 148.
5. Buechner, 254.

10. THE PRISON OF MY OWN CREATION

1. *Webster's Ninth New Collegiate Dictionary* (Springfield, MA: Merriam-Webster, Inc., Publishers, 1987), 453.
2. Cassandra King Conroy, *Tell Me A Story: My Life with Pat Conroy* (New York: William Morrow, 2019), 144.

11. THE SINGLE GARMENT OF DESTINY

1. Samuel T. Lloyd III, *Sermons from the National Cathedral: Soundings for the Journey* (New York: Rowman & Littlefield Publishers, Inc., 2013), 319.
2. *Ibid.*
3. Mark Oakley, *By Way of the Heart: The Seasons of Faith* (London: Canterbury Press, 2019), 79.
4. *Ibid.*, 78.
5. *Ibid.*, 79
6. Angus Ritchie, "Pentecost (Whit Sunday)." *Church Times,* 21 May 2020. https://www.churchtimes.co.uk/articles/2020/29-may/faith/Sunday-s-read ings/pentecost-w-...
7. Lloyd, xii.

12. THE PORTRAIT OF GOD WE CALL THE TRINITY

1. Mark Oakley, *By Way of the Heart: The Seasons of Faith* (London: Canterbury Press, 2019), 82.
2. Martyn Percy, "Trinity Sunday." *The Bright Field: Meditations and Reflections for Ordinary Time.* Martyn Percy, Editor (London: Canterbury Press, 2014), 203.

3. *Ibid.*
4. Oakley, 82.

13. GUT-LEVEL COMPASSION

1. Craig L. Blomberg, *Matthew*. The New American Commentary, Vol. 22. David S. Dockery, General Editor (Nashville, TN: B&H Publishing Group1992), 166.
2. *The Book of Common Prayer* (New York: The Seabury Press, 1979), 355.
3. Angus Ritchie, "1st Sunday after Trinity." *Church Times*, 04 June 2020. https://www.churchtimes.co.uk/articles/2020/12-june/faith/sunday-s-readings/1st-sundayaft...
4. John Barton, "An Archbishop Led by the Spirit." *Church Times*, 05 June 2020. https://www.churchtimes.co.uk/articles/2020/5-june/faith/comment/opinion
5. *Ibid.*

14. OUR REMEDY IS THE GRACE OF CHRIST

1. N. T. Wright, *Matthew for Everyone: Part One, Chapters 1-15*. Second Edition. (Louisville, KY: Westminster John Knox Press, 2004), 137.
2. Robert H. Mounce, *Matthew*. New International Biblical Commentary. W. Ward Gasque, New Testament Editor (Peabody, MA: Hendrickson Publishers, LLC, 1991), 108.

15. DIFFERENT FACETS OF GOD'S GLORY

1. William Barclay, *The Parables of Jesus* (Louisville, KY: Westminster John Knox Press, 1999), 41.
2. John 8:7
3. Barclay, 40.
4. David McCullough, *John Adams* (New York: Simon and Schuster Paperbacks, 2001), 285.
5. N. T. Wright, *Matthew for Everyone: Part One, Chapters 1-15*. Second Edition (Louisville, KY: Westminster John Knox Press, 2004), 172.

16. THE LIVING TABLETS OF OUR HEARTS

1. C. H. Dodd, *The Epistle of Paul to the Romans*. The Moffatt New Testament Commentary. James Moffatt, Editor (New York: Harper and Brothers Publishers, 1932), 147.

2. Leander E. Keck, "The Letter of Paul to the Romans." *The HarperCollins Study Bible*. Wayne A. Meeks, General Editor (New York: HarperCollins, Publishers, Inc., 1993), 2116.

3. C. K. Barrett, *The Epistle to the Romans*. Harper's New Testament Commentaries. Henry Chadwick, General Editor (New York: Harper & Row Publishers, 1957), 172.

4. Beverly Roberts Gaventa, *When In Romans: An Invitation to Linger with the Gospel According to Paul* (Grand Rapids, MI: Baker Academic, 2016), 114.

5. N. T. Wright, *Paul for Everyone: Romans, Part One, Chapters 1-8*. (Louisville, KY: Westminster John Knox Press, 2004), 159.

6. David M. Kasali, "Romans." *Africa Bible Commentary*. Tokunboh Adeyemo, General Editor (Grand Rapids, MI: Zondervan, 2006), 1390.

7. Barrett, 171.

8. *Ibid.*

9. Wright, 159.

17. FOR THERE IS NO DISTINCTION

1. C. H. Dodd, *The Epistle of Paul to the Romans*. The Moffatt New Testament Commentary. James Moffatt, Editor (New York and London: Harper and Brothers Publishers, 1932), 169.

2. Matthew Black, *Romans*. The New Century Bible Commentary. Ronald E. Clements and Matthew Black, General Editors (Grand Rapids, MI: William B. Eerdmans Publishing Company, 1973), 139.

18. HOLDING HER GROUND

1. Robert H. Mounce, *Matthew*. New International Biblical Commentary. W. Ward Gasque, New Testament Editor (Peabody, MA: Hendrickson Publishers, 1991), 153.

2. Angus Ritchie, "10th Sunday after Trinity." *Church Times*, 06 August 2020. https://.www.churchtimes.co.uk/articles/2020/14-august/faith/sunday-s-readings/10th-sund...

3. Margaret Davies, *Matthew* (Sheffield, England: JSOT Press, 1993), 115.

4. Amy-Jill Levine, "Gospel of Mathew." *Women's Bible Commentary*. Third Edition. Carol A. Newsom, Sharon H. Ringe and Jacqueline E. Lapsley, Editors (Louisville, KY: Westminster John Knox Press, 2012), 474.

5. *Ibid.*

6. Rob Gieselmann, *Irony and Jesus: Parables, Miracles and Stories* (Berkeley, CA: The Apocryphile Press, 2019), 81.

19. THE WORLD OF GRACE

1. James D. G. Dunn, *Romans 9-16*. Word Biblical Commentary, Volume 38B. Bruce M. Metzger, David A. Hubbard and Glenn W. Barker, General Editors (Grand Rapids, MI: Zondervan, 1988), 739.
2. *Ibid.*, 740.
3. *Ibid.*, 752.
4. *Ibid.*, 741.
5. *Ibid.*, 753.
6. N.T. Wright, *Paul for Everyone: Romans, Part Two, Chapters 9-16*. (Louisville, KY: Westminster John Knox Press, 2004), 80.
7. N. T. Wright, *Twelve Months of Sundays: Biblical Meditations on the Christian Years A, B & C* (New York: Morehouse Publishing, 2000), 101.
8. Dunn, 756.
9. "Jacob Blake's Mother Says Son Would Be 'Unpleased' by Response to Kenosha Shooting." https://www.nbcchicago.com/news/local/jacob-blakes-mother-sa...8/28/2020.
10. *Ibid.*

20. A LOVE THAT IS NOT EASY

1. N. T. Wright, *Paul for Everyone: Romans, Part Two, Chapters 9-16*. (Louisville, KY: Westminster John Knox Press, 2004), 93.
2. David M. Kasali, "Romans." *Africa Bible Commentary*. Tokunboh Adeyemo, General Editor (Grand Rapids, MI: Zondervan, 2006), 1398.
3. *The Book of Common Prayer* (New York: The Seabury Press, 1979), 305.
4. Michael Leunig, *A Common Prayer* (North Blackburn, Victoria, Australia: Collins Dove, 1990), 64.

21. AN EXTRAORDINARY PORTRAIT OF GRACE

1. Joel W. Rosenberg, "Genesis." *The HarperCollins Study Bible*. Wayne A. Meeks, General Editor (New York: HarperCollins, Publishers, Inc., 1993), 55.
2. Gerhard von Rad, *Genesis*. The Old Testament Library. Revised Edition. Peter Ackroyd, James Barr, Bernhard W. Anderson and James L. Mays, General Editors (Philadelphia, PA: The Westminster Press, 1972), 435.
3. Rosenberg, 55.
4. John A. Sanford, *The Man Who Wrestled with God: Light from the Old Testament on the Psychology of Individuation* (New York: Paulist Press, 1974), 72.
5. von Rad, 435.
6. *Ibid.*, 437.
7. Barnabe Assohoto and Samuel Ngewa, "Genesis." *African Bible Commentary*. Tokunboh Adeyemo, General Editor (Grand Rapids, MI: Zondervan,

2006), 84.

8. Angus Ritchie, "14th Sunday after Trinity." *Church Times*, 03 September 2020. https://www.churchtimes.co.uk/articles/2020/11-september/faith...

9. *The Book of Common Prayer* (New York: The Seabury Press, 1979), 305.

22. THE WIDENESS OF GOD'S MERCY

1. Craig L. Blomberg, *Matthew*. The New American Commentary, Volume 22. David S. Dockery, General Editor (Nashville, TN: B & H Publishing Group, 1992), 304.
2. Archibald M. Hunter, *Interpreting the Parables* (Philadelphia: The Westminster Press, 1960), 52.
3. *Ibid.*, 54.
4. Stephen Wright, *Tales Jesus Told: An Introduction to the Narrative Parables of Jesus* (Waynesboro, GA: Paternoster Press, 2002), 113.
5. John Claypool, *Stories Jesus Still Tells: The Parables*. Revised Second Edition (Cambridge, MA: Cowley Publications, 2000), 27.
6. *Ibid.*, 32.
7. *Ibid.*, 33.
8. Br. David Steindl-Rast, *Gratefulness, the Heart of Prayer: An Approach to Life in Fullness* (New York: Paulist Press, 1984), 12.

23. GOTTA SERVE SOMEBODY

1. Italo Calvino, *The Uses of Literature* (San Diego, CA: Harcourt Brace Jovanovich, 1986), 128.
2. Gabrielle Earnshaw, *Henri Nouwen & The Return of the Prodigal Son: The Making of a Spiritual Classic* (Brewster, MA: Paraclete Press, 2020), 138.
3. N. T. Wright, *Twelve Months of Sundays: Biblical Meditations on the Christian Years A, B & C* (New York: Morehouse Publishing, 2000), 109.
4. N. T. Wright, *Paul for Everyone: The Prison Letters*. Second Edition. (Louisville, KY: Westminster John Knox Press, 2004), 102.
5. Fred B. Craddock, *The Cherry Log Sermons* (Louisville, KY: Westminster John Knox Press, 2001), 92.
6. Ralph P. Martin, *Philippians*. Second Edition. Tyndale New Testament Commentaries, Vol. 11. Leon Morris, General Editor (Downers Grove, IL: IVP Academic, 1987), 101.
7. Richard R. Melick, Jr., *Philippians, Colossians, Philemon*. The New American Commentary, Vol. 32. David S. Dockery, General Editor (Nashville, TN: B & H Publishing Group, 1991), 95.
8. Jeffrey Munroe, *Reading Buechner: Exploring the Work of a Master Memoirist, Novelist, Theologian, and Preacher* (Downers Grove, IL: InterVarsity Press, 2019), 106.

24. A LIVING TEXT

1. Michael Mayne, *A Year Lost and Found*. Second Edition (London: Darton, Longman and Todd Ltd., 2007), 2.
2. D. Michael Martin, *1, 2 Thessalonians*. The New American Commentary, Volume 33. E. Ray Clendenen, General Editor (Nashville, TN: B&H Publishing Group, 1995), 81.
3. Monya A. Stubbs, "1 Thessalonians." *Women's Bible Commentary*. Third Edition. Carol A. Newsom, Sharon H. Ringe and Jacqueline E. Lapsley, Editors (Louisville, KY: Westminster John Knox Press, 2012), 590.
4. Martin, 81.
5. Angus Ritchie, "Last Sunday after Trinity." *Church Times*, 5 October 2020. https://www.churchtimes.co.uk/articles/2020/23-october/faith/s...

25. THE JOYFUL SERVICE OF THOSE IN NEED

1. *The Book of Common Prayer* (New York: The Seabury Press, 1979), 308.
2. Angus Ritchie, "All Saints' Day." *Church Times*, 22 October 2020. https://www.churchtimes.co.uk/articles/2020/30-october/faith/s...
3. *Ibid.*
4. Amy-Jill Levine, "Matthew." *Women's Bible Commentary*. Third Edition. Carol A. Newsom, Sharon H. Ringe and Jacqueline E. Lapsley, Editors (Louisville, KY: Westminster John Knox Press, 2012), 469.
5. Bert Ghezzi, *Voices of the Saints: A Year of Readings* (New York: Image Books/Doubleday, 2000), xviii.

27. A MIX OF PAIN AND HOPE

1. *The Book of Common Prayer* (New York: The Seabury Press, 1979), 717.
2. David McCullough, *John Adams* (New York: Simon and Schuster Paperbacks, 2001), 285.
3. Nancy L. Declaissé-Walford, "Psalms." *Women's Bible Commentary*. Third Edition. Carol A. Newson, Sharon H. Ringe and Jacqueline E. Lapsley, Editors (Louisville, KY: Westminster John Knox Press, 2012), 229.
4. Mitchell Dahood, *Psalms II:51-100*. The Anchor Bible. William Foxwell Albright and David Noel Freedman, General Editors (Garden City, NY: Doubleday and Company, Inc., 1968), 322.

28. TRULY I TELL YOU

1. Fleming Rutledge, *Advent: The Once and Future Coming of Jesus Christ* (Grand Rapids, MI: William B. Eerdmans Publishing Company, 2018), 231.
2. Fred B. Craddock, *The Collected Sermons of Fred B. Craddock* (Louisville, KY: Westminster John Knox Press, 2011), 95.
3. *Ibid.*
4. *Ibid.*, 96.
5. Rutledge, 234.
6. Carol Harrison, "Christ the King." *Untamed Gospel: Protests, Poems and Prose for the Christian Year.* Martyn Percy, Editor (London: Canterbury Press, 2017), 102.
7. Sam Keen, *Hymns to an Unknown God: Awakening the Spirit in Everyday Life* (New York: Bantam Books, 1994), 59.

29. ATTENTION

1. Fleming Rutledge, *Advent: The Once and Future Coming of Jesus Christ* (Grand Rapids, MI: William B. Eerdmans Publishing Company, 2018), 265.
2. *Ibid.*, 264.
3. *Ibid.*, 270.
4. Michael Mayne, *To Trust and to Love: Sermons and Addresses.* Joel W. Huffstetler, Editor (London: Darton, Longman and Todd Ltd, 2013), 5.

31. IT MAKES A DIFFERENCE WHAT YOU BELIEVE

1. Fred. B. Craddock, *John.* Knox Preaching Guides. John H. Hayes, Editor (Atlanta, GA: John Knox Press, 1982.), 11.
2. Barbara Brown Taylor, "The Gift of John's Cosmic Retelling." *Church Times,* 18 December 2020. https://www.churchtimes.co.uk/articles/2020/18-december/feat...
3. *Webster's Ninth New Collegiate Dictionary* (Springfield, MA: Merriam-Webster Inc., Publishers, 1987), 294.
4. *Ibid.*
5. N. T. Wright, *John for Everyone: Part One, Chapters 1-10.* Second Edition (Louisville, KY: Westminster John Knox Press, 2004), 3.
6. Craddock, 8.
7. *Ibid.*
8. *Ibid.*, 10.
9. *Ibid.*, 12.

BIBLIOGRAPHY

Assohoto, Barnabe, and Samuel Ngewa. "Genesis." *Africa Bible Commentary*. Tokunboh Adeyemo, General Editor. Grand Rapids, MI: Zondervan, 2006.

Barclay, William. *The Gospel of Matthew: Volume 1*. Revised Edition. The Daily Bible Study Series, Louisville, KY: Westminster John Knox Pres, 1975.

_____ *The Parables of Jesus*. Louisville, KY: Westminster John Knox Press, 1999.

Barrett, C. K. *The Epistle to the Romans*. Harper's New Testament Commentaries. Henry Chadwick, General Editor. New York: Harper & Row, Publishers, 1957.

Barton, John. "An Archbishop Led by the Spirit." *Church Times*, 05 June 2020. https://www.churchtimes.co.uk/articles/2020/5-June/comment/opinion/...

Black, Matthew. *Romans*. The New Century Bible commentary. Ronald E. Clements and Matthew Black, General Editors. Grand Rapids, MI: William B. Eerdmans Publishing Company, 1973.

Blomberg, Craig L. *Matthew*. The New American Commentary, Volume 22. David S. Dockery, General Editor. Nashville, TN: B & H Publishing Group, 1992.

The Book of Common Prayer. New York: The Seabury Press, 1979.

Bruce, F. F. *Philippians*. New International Biblical Commentary. W. Ward Gasque, New Testament Editor. Peabody, MA: Hendrickson Publishers, Inc., 1989.

Buechner, Frederick. *Secrets In the Dark: A Life in Sermons*. New York: HarperSanFrancisco, 2006.

Burdick, Donald W., and John H. Skilton. "1 Peter." *NASB Study Bible*. Kenneth L. Barker, General Editor. Grand Rapids, MI: Zondervan, 1999.

Burridge, Richard A. *John: A Guide for Reflection and Prayer.* Daily Bible Commentary. Peabody, MA: Hendrickson Publishers, Inc.., 1998.

"C. S. Lewis on the Past as a Foreign Country." April 5, 2013. https://faithandamericanhistory.wordpress.com/2013/04/05c-s-lewis-o...

Calvino, Italo. *The Uses of Literature.* San Diego, CA: Harcourt Brace Jovanovich, 1986.

Claypool, John. *Stories Jesus Still Tells: The Parables.* Revised Second Edition. Cambridge, MA: Cowley Publications, 2000.

Conroy, Cassandra King. *Tell Me A Story: My Life with Pat Conroy.* New York: William Morrow, 2019.

Craddock, Fred B. *The Cherry Log Sermons.* Louisville, KY: Westminster John Knox Press, 2001

_____ *The Collected Sermons of Fred B. Craddock.* Louisville, KY: Westminster John Knox Press, 2011.

_____ *John.* Knox Preaching Guides. John H. Hayes, Editor. Atlanta, GA: John Knox Press, 1982,

Dahood, Mitchell. *Psalms II:51-100.* The Anchor Bible. William Foxwell Albright and David Noel Freedman, General Editors. Garden City, NY: Doubleday and Company, Inc., 1968.

Davies, Margaret. *Matthew.* Sheffield (UK): JSOT Press, 1993.

Declaissé-Walford, Nancy L. "Psalms." *Women's Bible Commentary.* Third Edition. Carol A. Newsom, Sharon H. Ringe and Jacqueline E. Lapsley, Editors. Louisville, KY: Westminster John Knox Press, 2012.

Dodd, C. H. *The Epistle of Paul to the Romans.* The Moffatt New Testament Commentary. James Moffatt, Editor. New York and London: Harper and Brothers Publishers, 1932.

Duling, Dennis C. "The Gospel According to Matthew." *The HarperCollins*

Study Bible. Wayne E. Meeks, General Editor. New York: HarperCollins, Publishers, Inc., 1993.

Dunn, James D. G. *Romans 9-16.* Word Biblical Commentary, Volume 38B. Bruce M. Metzger, David A. Hubbard and Glenn W. Barker, General Editors. Grand Rapids, MI: Zondervan, 1988.

Earnshaw, Gabrielle. *Henri Nouwen & The Return of the Prodigal Son: The Making of a Spiritual Classic.* Brewster, MA: Paraclete Press, 2020.

Escobar, Kathy. *A Weary World: Reflections for a Blue Christmas.* Louisville, KY: Westminster John Knox Press, 2020.

Gaventa, Beverly Roberts. *When In Romans: An Invitation to Linger with the Gospel According to Paul.* Grand Rapids, MI: Baker Academic, 2016.

Gench, Frances Taylor. *Encounters with Jesus: Studies in the Gospel of John.* Louisville: KY: Westminster John Knox Press, 2007.

Ghezzi, Bert. *Voices of the Saints: A Year of Readings.* New York: Image Books/Doubleday, 2000.

Gieselmann, Rob. *Irony and Jesus: Parables, Miracles and Stories.* Berkeley, CA: The Apocryphile Press, 2019.

Hagner, Donald A. *Matthew 14-28.* Word Biblical Commentary, Volume 33B. Bruce M. Metzger, David A. Hubbard and Glenn W. Barker, General Editors. Nashville, TN: Thomas Nelson Publishers, 1995.

Harrison, Carol. "Christ the King." *Untamed Gospel: Protests, Poems and Prose for the Christian Year.* Martyn Percy, Editor. London: Canterbury Press, 2017.

Hatchett, Marion J. *Commentary on the American Prayer Book.* New York: The Seabury Press, 1980.

Holladay, Carl R. "Acts." *Harper's Bible Commentary.* James L. Mays, General Editor. San Francisco, CA: Harper & Row, Publishers, 1988.

_____ *Acts: A Commentary.* The New Testament Library. C. Clifton Black, M.

Eugene Boring and John T. Carroll, Editorial Advisory Board. Louisville, KY: Westminster John Knox Press, 2016.

Hunter, Archibald M. *Interpreting the Parables*. Philadelphia, PA: The Westminster Press, 1960.

Hylen, Susan E. *Imperfect Believers: Ambiguous Characters in the Gospel of John*. Louisville, KY: Westminster John Knox Press, 2009.

Johnson, Luke Timothy. *The Acts of the Apostles*. Sacra Pagina, Volume 5. Daniel J. Harrington, S. J., Editor. Collegeville, MN: The Liturgical Press, 1992.

Kähler, Martin. *The So-Called Historical Jesus and the Historic Biblical Christ*. Fortress Texts in Modern Theology. Edited and Translated by Carl. E. Braaten. Philadelphia, PA: Fortress Press, 1964.

Kapolyo, Joe. "Matthew." *Africa Bible Commentary*. Tokunboh Adeyemo, General Editor. Grand Rapids, MI: Zondervan, 2006.

Kasali, David M. "Romans." *Africa Bible Commentary*. Tokunboh Adeyemo, General Editor. Grand Rapids, MI: Zondervan, 2006.

Käsemann, Ernst. Commentary on Romans. Edited and translated by Geoffrey W. Bromiley. Grand Rapids, MI: William B. Eerdmans Publishing Company, 1980.

Keats, John. Letter to George and Georgianna Keats. February 14, 1818.

Keck, Leander E. "The Letter of Paul to the Romans." *The HarperCollins Study Bible*. Wayne A. Meeks, General Editor. New York: HarperCollins Publishers, Inc., 1993.

Keen, Sam. *Hymns to an Unknown God: Awakening the Spirit in Everyday Life*. New York: Bantam Books, 1994.

Keener, Craig S. *The Gospel of Matthew: A Socio-Rhetorical Commentary*. Grand Rapids: MI: William B. Eerdmans Publishing Company, 2009.

Kruse, Colin G. *Paul's Letter to the Romans.* The Pillar New Testament. D. A. Carson, General Editor. Grand Rapids, MI: William B. Eerdmans Publishing Company, 2012.

Kysar, Robert. *John: The Maverick Gospel.* Revised Edition. Louisville, KY. Westminster John Knox Press, 1993.

Leunig, Michael. *A Common Prayer.* North Blackburn, Victoria (Australia): Collins Dove, 1990.

Levine, Amy-Jill. "Matthew." *Women's Bible Commentary.* Third Edition. Carol A. Newsom, Sharon H. Ringe and Jacqueline E. Lapsley, Editors. Louisville, KY: Westminster John Knox Press, 2012.

_____ *Short Stories by Jesus: The Enigmatic Parables of A Controversial Rabbi.* New York: HarperOne, 2014.

Lloyd, Samuel T. *Sermons from the National Cathedral: Soundings for the Journey.* New York: Rowman and Littlefield Publishers, Inc., 2013.

McCullough, David. *John Adams.* New York: Simon & Schuster Paperbacks, 2001.

Martin, D. Michael. *1, 2 Thessalonians.* The New American Commentary, Volume 33. E. Ray Clendenen, General Editor. Nashville, TN: B & H Publishing Group, 1995.

Martin, Ralph P. *Philippians.* Second Edition. Tyndale New Testament Commentaries, Volume 11. Leon Morris, General Editor. Downers Grove, IL: IVP Academic, 1987.

Mayne, Michael. *A Year Lost and Found.* Second Edition. London: Darton, Longman and Todd, Ltd., 2007.

_____ *Dust that Dreams of Glory: Reflections on Lent and Holy Week.* Joel W. Huffstetler, Editor. London: Canterbury Press, 2017.

_____ *Responding to the Light: Reflections on Advent, Christmas and Epiphany.* Joel W. Huffstetler, Editor. London: Canterbury Press, 2017.

_____ *To Trust and to Love: Sermons and Addresses*. Joel W. Huffstetler, Editor. London: Darton, Longman and Todd., Ltd., 2010.

Melick, Jr., Richard R. *Philippians, Colossians, Philemon*. The New American Commentary, Volume 32. David S. Dockery, General Editor. Nashville, TN: B & H Publishing Group, 1991.

Moessner, David P. "Reading Luke's Gospel as Ancient Hellenistic Narrative: Luke's Narrative Plan of Israel's Suffering Messiah as God's Saving Plan for the World." *Reading Luke: Interpretation, Reflection, Formation*. Scripture and Hermeneutics Series, Volume 6. Craig G. Bartholomew, Joel B. Green and Anthony C.Thiselton, Editors. Grand Rapids, MI: Zondervan, 2005.

Morris, Leon. *The Gospel According to Matthew*. The Pillar New Testament Commentary. D. A. Carson, General Editor. Grand Rapids, MI: William B. Eerdmans Publishing Company, 1992.

Mounce, Robert H. *Matthew*. New International Biblical Commentary. W. Ward Gasque, New Testament Editor. Peabody, MA: Hendrickson Publishers, 1991.

Munrow, Jeffrey. *Reading Buechner: Exploring the Work of a Master Memoirist, Novelist, Theologian, and Preacher*. Downers Grove, IL: InterVarsity Press, 2019.

The NASB Study Bible. Kenneth Barker, General Editor. Grand Rapids, MI: Zondervan Publishing House, 1991.

Neil, William. *The Acts of the Apostles*. The New Century Bible Commentary. Ronald E. Clements and Matthew Black, General Editors. Grand Rapids, MI: William B. Eerdmans Publishing company, 1973.

The New English Bible (New Testament). Donald Ebor, Chairman of the Joint Commission. New York: Oxford University Press, 1961.

Oakley, Mark. *By Way of the Heart: The Seasons of Faith*. London: Canterbury Press, 2019.

O'Day, Gail R. "Gospel of John." *Women's Bible commentary*. Third Edition. Carol A. Newsom, Sharon H. Ringe and Jacqueline E. Lapsley, Editors. Louisville, KY: Westminster John Knox Press, 2012.

O'Day, Gail R., and Susan E. Hylen. *John.* Westminster Bible Commentary. Patrick D. Miller and David L. Bartlett, Series Editors. Louisville, KY: Westminster John Knox Press, 2006.

Percy, Martyn. *The Bright Field: Meditations and Reflections for Ordinary Time.* Martyn Percy, Editor. London: Canterbury Press, 2019.

Polhill, John B. *Acts.* The New American Commentary, Volume 26. David S. Dockery, General Editor. Nashville, TN: B & H Publishing Group, 1992.

Proust, Marcel. "Marcel Proust Quotes." https://www.brainyquote.-com/quotes/marcel_proust_107111.

Ritchie, Angus. "1st Sunday after Trinity." *Church Times,* 04 June 2020. https://www.churchtimes.co.uk/articles/2020/12-june/faith/sunday-s-readings/1st-sunday-aft...

_____ "3rd Sunday after Trinity." *Church Times,* 18 June 2020. https://www.churchtimes.co.uk/articles/2020/26-june/faith/sunday-s-readings/3rd-sunday-a...

_____ "5th Sunday after Trinity." *Church Times,* 02 July 2020. https://www.churchtimes.co.uk/articles/2020/10-july/faith/sunday-s-readings/5th-sunday-a...

_____ "10th Sunday after Trinity." *Church Times,* 06 August 2020. https://www.churchtimes.co.uk/articles/2020/14-august/faith/sunday-s-readings/10th-sund...

_____ "14th Sunday after Pentecost." *Church Times,* 03 September 2020. https://www.churchtimes.co.uk/articles/2020/11-september/faith/s...

_____ "All Saints Day." *Church Times,* 22 October 2020. https://www.churchtimes.co.uk/articles/2020/30-october/faith/s...

_____ "Last Sunday after Trinity." *Church Times,* 15 October 2020. https://www.churchtimes.co.uk/articles/2020/23-october/faith/s...

_____ "Pentecost (Whit Sunday)." *Church Times,* 21 May 2020.

https://www.churchtimes.co.uk/articles/2020/29-may/faith/Sunday-s-readings/pentecost-w...

Rohr, Richard. *Preparing for Christmas: Daily Meditations for Advent.* Cincinnati, OH: Franciscan Media, 2008.

Rosenberg, Joel W. "Genesis." *The HarperCollins Study Bible.* Wayne A. Meeks, General Editor. New York: HarperCollins, Publishers, Inc., 1993.

Rutledge, Fleming. *Advent: The Once and Future Coming of Jesus Christ.* Grand Rapids, MI: William B. Eerdmans Publishing Company, 2018.

_____ *The Undoing of Death: Sermons for Holy Week and Easter.* Grand Rapids, MI: William B. Eerdmans Publishing Company, 2002.

Sanford, John A. *The Man Who Wrestled with God: Light from the Old Testament on the Psychology of Individuation.* New York: Paulist Press, 1974

Spencer, Aída Besançon. *2 Corinthians: A Guide for Reflection and Prayer.* Daily Bible Commentary. Peabody, MA: Hendrickson Publishers, Inc., 2001.

Steindl-Rast, David. *Gratefulness, the Heart of Prayer: An Approach to Life in Fullness.* New York: Paulist Press, 1984.

Taylor, Barbara Brown. "The Gift of John's Cosmic Retelling." *Church Times.* 18 December 2020. https://www.churchtimes.co.uk/articles/2020/18-december/feat...

von Rad, Gerhard. *Genesis.* Second Edition. The Old Testament Library. Peter Ackroyd, James Barr, Bernhard Anderson and James L. Mays, General Editors. Philadelphia, PA: The Westminster Press, 1972.

Webster's Ninth New Collegiate Dictionary. Springfield, MA: Merriam-Webster, Inc., Publishers, 1987.

Williams, C. S. C. *A Commentary on the Acts of the Apostles.* Harper's New Testament Commentaries. Henry Chadwick, General Editor. Peabody, MA: Hendrickson Publishers, 1964.

Willimon, William H. *Acts*. Interpretation: A Bible Commentary for Teaching and Preaching. James L. Mays, Editor. Atlanta: John Knox Press, 1988.

Wright, N. T. *John for Everyone: Part One, Chapters 1-10*. Second Edition. Louisville, KY: Westminster John Knox Press, 2004.

_____ *Matthew for Everyone: Part One, Chapters 1-15*. Second Edition. Louisville, KY: Westminster John Knox Press, 2004.

_____ *Paul for Everyone: The Prison Letters*. Second Edition. Louisville, KY: Westminster John Knox Press, 2004.

_____ *Paul for Everyone: Romans, Part One, Chapters 1-8*. Louisville, KY: Westminster John Knox Press, 2004.

_____ *Paul for Everyone: Romans, Part Two, Chapters 9-16*. Louisville, KY: Westminster John Knox Press, 2004.

_____ *Twelve Months of Sundays: Biblical Meditations on the Christian Years A, B & C*. New York: Morehouse Publishing, 2000.

Wright, Stephen. *Tales Jesus Told: An Introduction to the Narrative Parables of Jesus*. Waynesboro, GA: Paternoster Press, 2002.

ABOUT THE AUTHOR

Joel W. Huffstetler is Rector of St. Luke's Episcopal Church in Cleveland, Tennessee. Ordained in 1990, he previously served as Assistant to the Rector of St. Paul's Episcopal Church, Chattanooga, Tennessee, and as Rector of St. Andrew's Episcopal Church in Canton, North Carolina. He is the author or editor of thirteen books, including *Practical Faith and Active Love: Meditations on the Epistle of James* (Apocryphile Press, 2020) and numerous articles and reviews.

Made in the USA
Middletown, DE
29 April 2023

29682272R00125